GROWING WISE IN FAMILY LIFE

BIBLE STUDY GUIDE

From the Bible-teaching ministry of

INSIGHT FOR LIVING

Charles R. Swindoll is a graduate of Dallas Theological Seminary and has served in pastorates for more than twenty-five years, including churches in Texas, New England, and California. Since 1971 he has served as senior pastor of the First Evangelical Free Church of Fullerton, California. Chuck's radio program, "Insight for Living," began in 1979. In addition to his church and radio ministries, Chuck enjoys writing. He has authored numerous books and booklets on a variety of subjects.

Based on the outlines of Chuck's sermons, the study guide text is coauthored by Ken Gire, a graduate of Texas Christian University and Dallas Theological Seminary. The Living Insights are written by Bill Butterworth, a graduate of Florida Bible College, Dallas Theological Seminary, and Florida Atlantic University. Ken Gire is presently the director of Insight for Living's Educational Products Department, and Bill Butterworth currently writes free-lance for the Educational Products Department.

Editor in Chief:
Cynthia Swindoll
Coauthor of Text:
Ken Gire
Author of Living Insights:
Bill Butterworth
Assistant Editor:
Karene Wells
Editorial Assistant:
Glenda Schlahta
Copy Manager:
Jac La Tour
Copyediting Supervisor:
Marty Anderson
Copy Editor:
Wendy Peterson

Director, Communications Division:
Carla Beck
Project Managers:
Alene Cooper and Nina Paris
Project Supervisor:
Cassandra Clark
Art Director:
Don Pierce
Production Artist:
Diana Vasquez
Typographer:
Bob Haskins
Print Production Manager:
Deedee Snyder
Printer:
Frye and Smith

Unless otherwise identified, all Scripture references are from the New American Standard Bible, © The Lockman Foundation 1960, 1962, 1963, 1968, 1971, 1972, 1973, 1975, 1977. Used by permission.

ISBN 0-88070-292-3

COVER DESIGN: Jenkins & Jenkins

Table of Contents

i

This study guide was written to correspond with the *Growing Wise in Family Life* cassette series. It also correlates, in part, with Chuck's book *Growing Wise in Family Life* (Portland, Oreg.: Multnomah Press, 1988). Chuck wrote the book after preaching the various series on which it is based. While writing the book, he decided to add some helpful material which was not originally included in his sermons. He also realized that there was too much material for one book, so he excluded some, which we, of course, left in the Insight for Living cassette series. Since we anticipate that some individuals will want to include the book in their study with the guide and cassettes, the following notes should help in understanding how all three interrelate.

1. The sermon "Danger Signals of a Disintegrating Family" was used in the development of the chapter "The Disintegrating Family: A Study in Tragedy," which also includes portions of "The Christian and the Family" given by Chuck at the Congress on the Bible II, September 25, 1987.

2. The sermon "Is Yours a Genuinely Christian Family?" was used in the development of the chapter "The Strong Family: Some Distinctive Marks," which also includes portions of "The Christian and the Family" given by Chuck at the Congress on the Bible II, September 25, 1987.

3. The sermon "Dads, Front and Center" was used in the development of the chapter "The Father: Masculine Model of Leadership."

4. The sermon "Mothers: An Endangered Species" was used in the development of the chapter "The Mother: Positive Partner of Support."

5. The sermon "Mom and Dad . . . Meet Your Child" was used in the development of the chapter "The Child: Your Baby Has the Bents!"

6. The sermon "The Bents in Your Baby" was also used in the development of the chapter "The Child: Your Baby Has the Bents!"

7. The sermon "A Chip off the Old Bent" does not appear as a chapter in the book.

8. The sermon "When Brothers and Sisters Battle," previously titled "The Scourge of Sibling Rivalry," does not appear as a chapter in the book.

9. The sermon "Shaping the Will with Wisdom" was used in the development of the chapter "Discipline: Shaping the Will with Wisdom."

10. The sermon "Ways to Enhance Esteem" was used in the development of the chapter "Affirmation: Enhancing Esteem."

11. The sermon "Change: Challenging Years of Adolescence," formerly titled "Adolescence: Challenging Years of Change," was used in the development of the chapter "Change: Challenging Years of Adolescence."

12. The sermon "Another Look at Adolescence" was also used in the development of the chapter "Change: Challenging Years of Adolescence."

13. The sermon "What's *Right* about Adolescence?" was used in the development of the chapter "Relationships: Having Fun with Your Family," which also includes material from the sermon "Another Look at Adolescence."

14. The sermon "You and Your Son" does not appear as a chapter in the book.

15. The sermon "You and Your Daughter" (Part One) does not appear as a chapter in the book.

16. The sermon "You and Your Daughter" (Part Two) does not appear as a chapter in the book.

17. The sermon "Releasing the Reins" does not appear as a chapter in the book.

18. The sermon "What about the Older Rebel?" was used in the development of the chapter "Confronting the Unpleasant."

19. The sermon "Equipping the Family for the Unforeseen" was used in the development of the chapter "Facing the Unforeseen."

20. The sermon "Equipping the Family for the Unbearable" was used in the development of the chapter "Enduring the Unbearable."

21. The sermon "Equipping the Family for the Unusual" was used in the development of the chapter "Anticipating the Unusual."

22. The sermon "What to Do When You've Blown It" was used in the development of the chapter "Accepting the Undeniable."

23. The sermon "Looking Back on Things That Matter" does not appear as a chapter in the book.

24. The sermon "Looking Ahead to Things That Last" does not appear as a chapter in the book.

Growing Wise in Family Life

Everything I read these days assures me that the family is "in." Many of the books, television shows, and movies now in the marketplace are centering attention on domestic scenes. Clearly, the "hot ticket" is family life.

But wait. Even though all this is true, who says that what is being portrayed on page and stage is accurate? The more we see of what is being produced by the secular media, the more we realize how unbiblical (and often how unwholesome) the material is. What good is it if the family is "in" but God's timeless wisdom is "out"? Seems to me that our need today is for fresh and forthright insight from our ever-relevant Lord, whose Word is still unsurpassed when it comes to reliable information.

That, in a nutshell, explains why I have chosen to prepare and present this study, which places proper emphasis on wisdom in family living. If my words of instruction bring you back to the principles of Scripture, causing you to discover biblical truth and how to put it into action, my goal will have been reached . . . my prayers will have been answered.

Chuck Swindoll

Putting Truth into Action

Knowledge apart from application falls short of God's desire for His children. Knowledge must result in change and growth. Consequently, we have constructed this Bible study guide with these purposes in mind: (1) to stimulate discovery, (2) to increase understanding, and (3) to encourage application.

At the end of each lesson is a section called **Living Insights.** *There you'll be given assistance in further Bible study, and you'll be encouraged to contemplate and apply the things you've learned. This is the place where the lesson is fitted with shoe leather for your walk through the varied experiences of life.*

It's our hope that you'll discover numerous ways to use this tool. Some useful avenues we suggest are personal meditation, joint discovery, and discussion with your spouse, family, work associates, friends, or neighbors. The study guide is also practical for Sunday school classes, Bible study groups, and, of course, as a study aid for the "Insight for Living" radio broadcast.

In order to derive the greatest benefit from this process, we suggest that you record your responses to the lessons in the space which has been provided for you. In view of the kinds of questions asked, your study guide may become a journal filled with your many discoveries and commitments. We anticipate that you will find yourself returning to it periodically for review and encouragement.

Ken Gire
Coauthor of Text

Bill Butterworth
Author of Living Insights

GROWING WISE IN
FAMILY LIFE

Section One:

WISDOM USED IN APPRAISING THE SCENE

Danger Signals of a Disintegrating Family
1 Samuel 1–4

The deterioration of a house, once teeming with life, is a tragic thing to see. Rafters sagging like slumped shoulders under the burden of decades. Ceilings mapped with remembered rain from shingles too weary to withstand the elements. Windows, once bursting with morning light, now silted over from neglect. A pall of somber, gray dust shrouding its derelict interior.

There are no voices in the old house. No lively talk over the dinner table. No laughter. Only an infrequent, musty wheeze from the attic . . . an occasional arthritic creak in the ceiling joists . . . a nostalgic sigh for memories past.

It's a sad sight.

But even more sad, more tragic, is the slow disintegration of a family. In this lesson, we'll witness one such family. And, hopefully, the signs of deterioration will stand out so glaringly as to motivate us to make the necessary repairs before our home suffers a similar fate.

I. Meet the Family
Turning back the yellowed pages of time, we come to an ancient account of a disintegrating family in 1 Samuel 1–4. Unfortunately, we see no pictures of the mother propped on this family's mantle. Instead, our eyes are drawn to a portrait of the father's relationship with his two natural sons and one adopted son.

A. The father: Eli. Next to that large center portrait sit three smaller pictures framing separate aspects of Eli's life—professional, personal, and physical—pictures that form a composite of this pillar in Israel's community. Like many respected men today, Eli was called upon to assume a position of leadership in the community. First and foremost was his role as high priest (1:9b). Besides his ceremonial role, Eli served in a civil capacity

1

as a judge—a position he occupied for forty years (4:18).[1] Added to these professional responsibilities, Eli also had the personal responsibility of being a father to two sons (1:3). As we view the third picture, we discover several physical qualities about Eli. In chapter 2, verse 22, we see that he "was very old." And attendant with that was failing vision (3:2b).[2] In 4:18 two more facts about Eli become visible—one negative, one positive.

> And it came about when [the messenger] mentioned the ark of God that Eli fell off the seat backward beside the gate, and his neck was broken and he died, for he was old and heavy. Thus he judged Israel forty years.

The man was severely overweight, a fact that contributed to his death. But, as a legacy, he left behind a forty-year record of faithful service—at least in regard to his professional life. He didn't fare so well, however, in his parental responsibilities.

B. The two natural sons: Hophni and Phinehas. Professionally, Eli's sons followed in their father's footsteps as priests (1:3b). Morally, however, they took a different path.

> The sons of Eli were worthless men; they did not know the Lord. (2:12)

The remainder of chapter 2 chronicles their cavalier attitude toward sin and their cynicism toward their spiritual duties. Not only did they not know the Lord, but they were unfamiliar with the priestly customs (vv. 13–17). And their personal lives, as well as their hearts, were far from God. So much so that they sinned blatantly by lying with "the women who served at the doorway of the tent of meeting" (v. 22b). Catching a gust of this gossip circulating among the people, Eli confronted his sons.

> And he said to them, "Why do you do such things, the evil things that I hear from all these people? No, my sons; for the report is not good which I hear the Lord's people circulating. If one man sins against another, God will mediate for him; but if a man sins against the Lord, who can intercede for him?" (vv. 23–25a)

Their response, however, revealed hearts that were stubborn and rebellious.

---

1. The tone of the passage and Eli's comments confirm his faith in God. In fact, his name literally means "Jehovah is high" or, more likely, "Jehovah-my God" (meaning, "Jehovah is my God").

2. Eli eventually went blind by age ninety-eight (1 Sam. 4:15). But despite the decline of his physical eyesight, his spiritual eyes were as sensitive as ever. When God was speaking to Samuel, Eli sensed it was the Lord and wisely instructed the young boy how to respond (3:8–9).

But they would not listen to the voice of their father,
for the Lord desired to put them to death. (v. 25b)

Calloused to Spiritual Things

Ephesians 4:18–19 describes Hophni and Phinehas to a
tee.

> Being darkened in their understanding, excluded
> from the life of God, because of the ignorance
> that is in them, because of the hardness of their
> heart; and they, having become callous, have
> given themselves over to sensuality, for the
> practice of every kind of impurity with greedi-
> ness.

When a person's heart resists spiritual truth, then that
truth is external to the person. And so, every rub that
person has with spiritual things does not spark a fire within
the heart, but forms a callus on the surface instead.

That's what every brush with their priestly responsibilities did to Hophni and Phinehas. They resisted truth, resented authority, and finally rebelled openly.

The same thing often happens with preachers' kids or
any children continually exposed to churchy talk, churchy
meetings, and churchy people. They go through the motions like a marionette on a string. They walk. They talk.
They bend at the joints. They look real, but inside is a
heart of wood. Someday they'll become cynical and cut
away the restricting strings.

We who are parents must ask ourselves: Are we making
our children into wooden puppets who dance on strings,
or are we helping them become real people who delight
in spiritual things? Are we lighting fires within their hearts,
or rubbing calluses on the surface?

C. The adopted son: Samuel. Born to Hannah and Elkanah as
a special gift from God, Samuel was given over to the Lord's
service in grateful response to His blessing (see 1 Sam. 1). Growing up in Eli's home, Samuel was raised by a foster father who
was passive, aging, overweight, and rapidly losing touch with
his children. On top of that, Samuel had to share the home with
two rebellious, older brothers. Like a fragrant flower planted in
a garbage dump, he stood in stark contrast to the moral stench
of Hophni and Phinehas. Yet, in this considerably less than ideal
soil, young Samuel flourished, serving the Lord (2:11) and developing into a strong young man.

Thus Samuel grew and the Lord was with him and
let none of his words fail. (3:19)

The Grace of the Gardener

Like a greenhouse on a garbage dump, God protected
and nurtured the tender spirit of Samuel. In the same way,
He can watch over the lives of your children.

Their home may be full of weeds. Their school may be
rocky soil. The moral climate around them may be tem-
pestuous.

God, however, is a remarkable gardener. And if we dedi-
cate our children to the Lord, no matter what garbage
dump they're on, He can put a greenhouse of grace around
them—and make something fruitful of their lives.

II. Observe the Activity

If we had lived down the street from Eli's house, we would have had
a pretty good idea of what went on there just by casting a glance
in that direction.

A. Sins of the sons. So shamelessly sinful were Hophni and
Phinehas that they engaged in flagrant immorality at the very
doorway of the tent of meeting (2:22). And "all Israel" was aware
of it. So repugnant was their rebellion and so wishy-washy was
their father's response that God finally stepped in with an irre-
versible judgment.

"For I have told him that I am about to judge his house
forever for the iniquity which he knew, because his
sons brought a curse on themselves and he did not
rebuke them." (3:13)

B. Warnings of others. If you read through the account, you
will find several categories of messengers that the Lord used to
warn of His impending intervention. The first warning was in
the form of a public report.

"No, my sons; for the report is not good which I hear
the Lord's people circulating." (2:24)

The second warning came from an unnamed prophet.

Then a man of God came to Eli and said to him,
". . . the Lord God of Israel declares, 'I did indeed say
that your house and the house of your father should
walk before Me forever'; but now the Lord declares,
'Far be it from Me—for those who honor Me I will
honor, and those who despise Me will be lightly es-
teemed. Behold, the days are coming when I will

4

break your strength and the strength of your father's house so that there will not be an old man in your house. And you will see the distress of My dwelling, in spite of all that I do good for Israel; and an old man will not be in your house forever. Yet I will not cut off every man of yours from My altar that your eyes may fail from weeping and your soul grieve, and all the increase of your house will die in the prime of life. And this will be the sign to you which shall come concerning your two sons, Hophni and Phinehas: on the same day both of them shall die.' " (vv. 27a, 30–34)

The final warning was from God Himself in the form of a vision to young Samuel.

And the Lord said to Samuel, "Behold, I am about to do a thing in Israel at which both ears of everyone who hears it will tingle. In that day I will carry out against Eli all that I have spoken concerning his house, from beginning to end." (3:11–12)

And Samuel, in turn, conveyed the prophecy to Eli (vv. 15–18).

Final Exams for Spiritual Leaders

The acid test of whether a pastor is qualified to lead a congregation is not a seminary degree ... not how many books he has published ... not how spellbinding his sermons are ... not how sophisticated his social skills are.

If not these, then what?

The true test of his ability to shepherd a flock is his report card at home. In fact, 1 Timothy 3:4–5 lists this as the *sine qua non* of a pastor:

He must be one who manages his own household well, keeping his children under control with all dignity (but if a man does not know how to manage his own household, how will he take care of the church of God?).

The point of the passage is basic: you don't make a flunking freshman academic dean of the college.

Such common sense. But so rarely applied when it comes to determining spiritual leadership.

C. **Response of the father.** Eli's way of dealing with his shameful sons was equivalent to a verbal slap on the hand—and a mild one at that.

And he said to them, "Why do you do such things, the evil things that I hear from all these people? No, my sons; for the report is not good which I hear the Lord's people circulating." (1 Sam. 2:23–24)
Eli was not only incomplete in his reproof, he even indulged his sons, as God's rebuke to him indicates.

" 'Why do you kick at My sacrifice and at My offering which I have commanded in My dwelling, and honor your sons above Me, by making yourselves fat with the choicest of every offering of My people Israel?' "
(v. 29)

By not intervening when they took such huge portions of meat for themselves, Eli was indulging his sons' sin. A final thing we note about Eli's response is a sort of passive fatalism. Note how he resigns himself when he hears Samuel's prophecy.

"It is the Lord; let Him do what seems good to Him."
(3:18)

Had Eli been obedient to the Law of Moses in the first place, he would have taken action that would have certainly prevented his sons from bringing such shame upon the family, the priesthood, and the nation (see Deut. 21:18–21).

III. Signs of Domestic Disintegration

OK, we've met the family and observed the activity in and around the home. Now it's time to do a little evaluating. What were some of the signs Eli ignored? What did he overlook? What was he blind to?

A. Preoccupation with his profession to the exclusion of his family's needs. Eli's intense focus on his responsibilities as priest and judge relegated his family to a blur in the background. No wonder he missed the faults in their formative years; they were never in focus in the first place. Alexander Whyte remarks:

Let me consider well how, conceivably, it could come about that Hophni and Phinehas could be born and brought up at Shiloh and not know the Lord? Well, for one thing, their father was never at home. What with judging all Israel, and what with sacrificing and interceding for all Israel, Eli never saw his children till they were in their beds. 'What mean ye by this ordinance?' all the other children in Israel asked at their fathers as they came up to the temple. And all the way up and all the way down again those fathers took their inquiring children by the hand and told them all about Abraham, and Isaac, and Jacob, and Joseph, and Moses, and Aaron, and the exodus, and the wilderness, and the conquest, and the yearly passover. Hophni and Phinehas were the only children in all Israel who saw the temple every day and paid no attention to it.[3]

B. Refusal to face the severity of his sons' lifestyle. When the reports of his sons' sin sharpened his focus, Eli refused to realize the gravity of the report. He must have ached inside—such a success at work and such a failure at home. Yet he rationalized away both the causes and the far-reaching consequences of his sons' actions. And so now his sons serve as examples to be avoided rather than emulated—trenchant illustrations of Proverbs 19:18:

> Discipline your son in his early years while there is hope. If you don't you will ruin his life.[4]

C. Failure to respond correctly to the warnings of others. God has ways of making the blind see—even parents who are blind to their children's faults. Sometimes His ways are miraculous; often, however, they are mundane. For He can use a teacher or a neighbor or a policeman. And yes, even a grandparent. How receptive are you when these people issue their warnings? How respectful? How appreciative? Do you listen, or do you get defensive? Remember the proverb:

> Where there is no guidance, the people fall,
> But in abundance of counselors there is victory. (11:14)

D. Condoning the wrong, thereby becoming a part of the problem. Take a closer look at a verse we saw earlier and see the Lord's stinging indictment.

> "'Why do you kick at My sacrifice and at My offering which I have commanded in My dwelling, and honor your sons above Me, by making yourselves fat with the choicest of every offering of My people Israel?'" (1 Sam. 2:29)

Notice the plural *yourselves.* Some of Eli's own weight came from adopting his sons' ways. He went from passive indifference to active indulgence. Centuries later the prophet Jeremiah, walking through the ruins of Jerusalem, lamented how sins are passed from one generation to another.

> Our fathers sinned, and are no more;
> It is we who have borne their iniquities. (Lam. 5:7)

Such is the recycled reality of sin. Yesterday's lunch, today's litter. And tomorrow's garbage will all stack up—on the family's front porch.

---

3. Alexander Whyte, *Bible Characters* (London, England: Oliphants, 1952), vol. 1, pp. 218–19.

4. The Living Bible (Wheaton, Ill.: Tyndale House Publishers, 1971).

Living Insights

Study One ━━━━━━━━━━━━━━━━━━━━━━━━━━━━━━━

As the title of this series suggests, we want to use these lessons to grow wise in our family life. Are you mentally prepared for this study? A good way to warm up for the race ahead is to take a few minutes to page through this study guide, getting a feel for the ground we'll be covering.

• To make this overview more manageable, skim through the first half of your study guide now. We'll look at the second half in our next study. As you read the titles and headings, use the following space to jot down some questions you anticipate getting answered during this series.

Anticipated Questions

_____

_____

_____

_____

_____

_____

_____

_____

_____

_____

_____

_____

_____

_____

_____

Living Insights

We're preparing ourselves for all that the series has to offer by scanning the lessons we'll be covering. Let's continue our pregame warm-up by looking over the second half.

● Glance through the last half of this study guide, once again looking for possible questions that might be answered in the lessons. Then write down your questions in the space provided.

Anticipated Questions

_____

_____

_____

_____

_____

_____

_____

_____

_____

_____

_____

_____

_____

_____

_____

_____

_____

Is Yours a Genuinely
Christian Family?
Deuteronomy 6:1–24

For millennia the eagle has stood as an august symbol of strength. Gliding high upon silent streams of air, the eagle, with its keen eyes, can detect even the slightest movement of a rodent. With its powerful pinions, it can swoop down to snatch the unsuspecting prey, using its strong talons to squeeze the life from its victim. And if the talons don't kill the animal, the eagle's sharp beak can break its neck or sever its head in an instant.

No wonder the eagle has been a symbol of power and strength since Babylonian days.

Yet most people don't know that the eagle has a strong sense of family. Eagles are monogamous, mate for life, and use the same nest year after year. To protect their young, they generally nest in inaccessible places, high in isolated trees or cliffs. Before the young eaglets can leave the nest on their own, they must wait three or four years for their adult plumage to grow. During that time, they are dutifully cared for by their parents.

But despite its superior strength and ability to survive, the North American bald eagle has become an endangered species. Pesticides, poachers, pollution, and the loss of natural nesting sites have been the culprits, severely depleting the population.

Although laws have now been passed to protect the bald eagle, concern was not registered until the eagle perched precariously on the brink of extinction.

Another symbol of strength—the family—also faces the danger of extinction. In today's lesson, we'll look at some ways to help it not only survive but soar.

I. Looking Ahead: The Challenge before Us
The author who gave us *Future Shock*, Alvin Toffler, later wrote a book titled *The Third Wave*. In it he looks ahead to the year 2000 and beyond. He contends that the first wave which rolled over the earth was an agricultural one. The second was the wave of industry. The third, which is now upon us, is the wave of technology. About this third wave he writes:

> A powerful tide is surging across much of the world today, creating a new, often bizarre, environment in which to work, play, marry, raise children, or retire. In this bewildering context, businessmen swim against highly erratic economic currents; politicians see their ratings bob

wildly up and down; universities, hospitals, and other institutions battle desperately against inflation. Value systems splinter and crash, while the lifeboats of family, church, and state are hurled madly about.[1]
We'll be swimming against the tide if we try to raise our families exactly as we were raised. The world is different today; but biblical principles haven't become extinct. So, if we're going to meet the challenge before us—that of maintaining strong families—we must look to the essentials within us.

II. Looking Within: The Essentials inside Us

As the Israelites prepared to enter Canaan, they, too, faced an intimidating challenge—to penetrate a pagan culture. To prepare them for that challenge, Moses took them aside, reiterating the essentials that would help their families not only survive but succeed (compare Deut. 6:24 with 6:2).[2]

A. Regarding the Lord our God. For Israel to survive successfully in the land, *parents had to be permeated by a love for God.*

"Now this is the commandment, the statutes and the judgments which the Lord your God has commanded me to teach you, that you might do them in the land where you are going over to possess it, so that you and your son and your grandson might fear the Lord your God, to keep all His statutes and His commandments, which I command you, all the days of your life, and that your days may be prolonged. O Israel, you should listen and be careful to do it, that it may be well with you and that you may multiply greatly, just as the Lord, the God of your fathers, has promised you, in a land flowing with milk and honey. Hear, O Israel! The Lord is our God, the Lord is one! And you shall love the Lord your God with all your heart and with all your soul and with all your might." (6:1–5)

Parents were to pass down to their children and grandchildren an awesome and healthy fear of God, an attentive ear to His voice, and a life of obedience (vv. 2–3a). This kind of all-encompassing love for God is authentic. You can't fake it. And parents who model this love will forever impact their children for good.

1. Alvin Toffler, *The Third Wave* (London, England: Pan Books, 1980), p. 15.

2. Deuteronomy, Moses' last words to the nation before they entered Canaan, literally means "second law" (from *deutero,* meaning "second" and *nomos,* meaning "law"). Essentially, the book is a repetition of previously revealed instructions, serving to underscore their importance. This, by the way, is why the Ten Commandments are listed twice, once in Exodus 20, and again in Deuteronomy 5.

B. Regarding the truth of His Word. For authenticity to be maintained in the home, there must be *a conscious, consistent transfer of God's truth to the young.* First, though, that truth must capture the heart of the parent.

> "And these words, which I am commanding you today, shall be on your heart." (v. 6)

Then a transfer takes place.

> "And you shall teach them diligently to your sons." (v. 7a)

As translated, the word *diligently* is an adverb. But in the Hebrew text, it is a verb that means "to sharpen."[3] The particular form of this verb in Hebrew intensifies the action. The sense then would be: "You shall *intensely* sharpen your sons." The teaching is not passive but aggressively active. The transfer of truth takes an investment of time and effort; it isn't automatic.

> "And [you] shall talk of them when you sit in your house and when you walk by the way and when you lie down and when you rise up." (v. 7b)

The Hebrew has terms for preaching and for lecturing, but neither term is used here. Instead, the word used simply means "talking." No formal lecture. No catechism. No rigid routine or Sunday school structure. Simply talking. Not just on Sunday. And not just at bedtime. But talking that takes place naturally during all times of the day, every day. Above all else, the home should be a place where God can be comfortably discussed in any conversation, at any time.

C. Regarding our response toward affluence. Entering Canaan—the land of milk and honey—the Israelites experienced the same temptations we do.

> "Then it shall come about when the Lord your God brings you into the land which He swore to your fathers, Abraham, Isaac and Jacob, to give you, great and splendid cities which you did not build, and houses full of all good things which you did not fill, and hewn cisterns which you did not dig, vineyards and olive trees which you did not plant, and you shall eat and be satisfied, then watch yourself, lest you forget the Lord who brought you from the land of Egypt, out of the house of slavery. You shall fear only the Lord your God; and you shall worship Him, and swear by His name. You shall not follow other gods, any of the gods of the peoples who surround you." (vv. 10–14)

3. The Hebrew term is *shanan.*

Suddenly, the Israelites would go from wilderness paupers to wealthy princes. Life would no longer be a Spartan diet of manna and quail, but a smorgasbord in the land of milk and honey. Canaan would be a cornucopia of fulfilled dreams. Luxurious homes. Sprawling estates. Botanical gardens. Fertile farmland. And what is the Lord's advice in the midst of all this affluence? To watch out, lest you forget to honor the Lord as the true source of all your blessings (see James 1:17). That brings us to another essential ingredient to keep family faith authentic: *a tender, humble heart of gratitude for God's provisions.* Observe that God doesn't say, "Don't live in those cities" or "You shouldn't have nice things" or "You shouldn't have it so easy." He merely says, "Watch out."

D. **Regarding the need for survival.** Deuteronomy 6:20–25 says that to ensure survival for individual families and for the nation as a whole, there must be *frequent, stated reminders of God's faithfulness and grace.*

> "When your son asks you in time to come, saying, 'What do the testimonies and the statutes and the judgments mean which the Lord commanded you?' then you shall say to your son, 'We were slaves to Pharaoh in Egypt; and the Lord brought us from Egypt with a mighty hand. Moreover, the Lord showed great and distressing signs and wonders before our eyes against Egypt, Pharaoh and all his household; and He brought us out from there in order to bring us in, to give us the land which He had sworn to our fathers.' So the Lord commanded us to observe all these statutes, to fear the Lord our God for our good always and for our survival, as it is today. And it will be righteousness for us if we are careful to observe all this commandment before the Lord our God, just as He commanded us."

When you're living authentic lives of faith, your children will be full of questions: "What does the Bible mean? Why do we believe it? Why don't we live like others around us?" And you'll find that the best answers are stated reminders of God's faithfulness and grace—telling your children what God has done in your life.

III. Looking Up: The Help above Us

The strong family is indeed an endangered species. But there is help from above when we are obedient to God in passing on His truth to our children. That truth is for their good . . . and for their survival. It's a matter of life and death, as another father reminded his son in Proverbs 6:20–23:

My son, observe the commandment of your father,
And do not forsake the teaching of your mother;
Bind them continually on your heart;
Tie them around your neck.
When you walk about, they will guide you;
When you sleep, they will watch over you;
And when you awake, they will talk to you.
For the commandment is a lamp, and the teaching is light;
And reproofs for discipline are the way of life.
When they have learned to follow your lead in their relationship
with the Lord, they will not only survive—they will gain new strength,
mount up with wings like eagles, and soar!

 Living Insights

Study One ▬▬▬▬▬▬▬▬▬▬▬▬▬▬▬▬▬▬▬▬▬▬▬▬▬▬▬▬▬▬▬

Deuteronomy 6 is the time-honored champion of truth in the arena
of family life. It may be a very familiar passage to you, or perhaps
you've never read it. Whichever the case, this text deserves further
study.

• The central passage in this chapter is verses 4–9. Rewrite those six
verses in your own words. This practice helps the serious student
of the Bible get deeper into the text by drawing out broader meanings and feelings beneath the words on the page. If you have the
time, go beyond verse 9 to the next paragraph, verses 10–15.

_____

_____

_____

_____

_____

_____

_____

_____

_____

Living Insights

One of the essentials for the strong family is a love for God that permeates the parent. Mom or Dad, does that phrase describe you? It can, you know. Let's give this issue to Him.

• Let's take this time to pray, asking God for strength, wisdom, and grace to help us renew our love for Him. We want to get closer to the Lord, allowing His truth to provide the direction in life we so desperately need. Talk to Him about your specific concerns and desires for your family.

WISDOM APPLIED TO CULTIVATING THE SOIL

Dads, Front and Center
1 Thessalonians 2:8–12

In his book *Promises to Peter,* Charlie Shedd tells how the title of his message on parenting changed with his experience of fatherhood. In his early years on the speaking circuit before he was a father, he called it "How to Raise Your Children." People came in droves to hear it. Then Charlie had a child, and it was a while before he gave that message again. When he did, it had a new name: "Some Suggestions to Parents." Two more children and a number of years later, he was calling it "Feeble Hints to Fellow Strugglers." Several years and children later, he seldom gave that talk. But when he did, his theme was "Anyone here got a few words of wisdom?"

It's tough being a dad. It's almost impossible to live up to our own standards, to say nothing of God's. And the toughest thing of all is that, deep inside, every father knows he is leaving an indelible thumbprint on the life of each of his children. Whether he's nuts-and-bolts practical or scrapes the Milky Way with his visionary ideas; whether he's strong and aggressive or weak and passive; whether he's a workaholic or an alcoholic—there's not a dad that doesn't know his fingerprints are all over his children as he molds and shapes them into the adults they will become.

How can fathers do this carefully and wisely? In this lesson we will take a few tips on parenting from the apostle Paul. We don't know if Paul was ever a father in the literal sense. But in his first letter to the Thessalonians, we see some fatherly characteristics that are well worth emulating.

I. A Little Background
The first two churches founded in Europe were in Philippi and Thessalonica. When Paul took a trip to Thessalonica, he saw potential in that city and wanted to stay, even though he was pursued and persecuted by unbelievers (see 1 Thess. 2:1–2). For six weeks, he poured himself into that handful of believers, working night and day to establish them in their newborn faith. Although Paul was never to return for another in-depth visit, the Thessalonian believers had captured his heart. So when he later heard about the waves of

persecution that threatened to drown their belief, he threw them two life preservers.

A. He sent Timothy to them. Unable to go to them himself, Paul sent his friend Timothy with words of hope and encouragement (3:2).

B. He wrote them a letter. When Timothy returned with a disheartening report, Paul wrote them an impassioned letter of exhortation. And pouring through his pen was a wellspring of love from a father's heart.

> But we proved to be gentle among you, as a nursing mother tenderly cares for her own children . . . imploring each one of you as a father would his own children. (2:7, 11b)

"As a . . . mother," "as a father"—these words appear nowhere else in Paul's writings. And it's in the context of Paul's fatherly heart that we draw some principles of parenting.

II. Five Guidelines for Good Dads

Verses 8–12 of chapter 2 paint an inspired portrait of a dad with his kids, one well worth copying.

A. A fond affection. The first quality Paul illustrates is affection: "Having thus a fond affection for you" (v. 8a). He had at his fingertips half a dozen Greek terms he could have used, but he picked a term that is found only this once in all the New Testament—a term that means "to feel oneself drawn to something or someone." It's a term of endearment taken from the nursery . . . a term both masculine and tender, the picture of a father gently cradling his tiny child. But how often do we really express this kind of "fond affection"? It's easy to hug and kiss a baby, even a small child. But as that child grows up, physical affection is often replaced with physical aloofness. Gordon MacDonald, in his book *The Effective Father,* includes a chapter called "Please Show Me That You Care." In it he writes:

> The physical expression of our approval is of great importance. We affirm what a person is, and we appreciate what a person does. But this assurance must be given in more than words. *Affection,* the nonverbal communication of closeness, touching, and stroking is among the most important experiences we share with one another.[1]

Research shows that sexual promiscuity in a woman can often be traced to a lack of fatherly affection in her childhood and

---

1. Gordon MacDonald, *The Effective Father* (Wheaton, Ill.: Tyndale House Publishers, 1977), p. 229. Used by permission.

adolescence.[2] Fathers, demonstrate your love—now, before your child starts looking for it elsewhere.

B. A transparent life. Verse 8 goes on to illustrate the second guideline: a transparent life.

> Having thus a fond affection for you, we were well-pleased to impart to you *not only the gospel of God but also our own lives,* because you had become very dear to us. (emphasis added)

Isn't the gospel important? Absolutely! And isn't it enough? Absolutely not! It's essential that your children hear the gospel if they are to come to know the Savior you love; and it's even better if the Good News comes from your own lips. But they need more than that. They need instruction about life, and they need a father who lets them watch him live it, mistakes and all. They need to see how you handle your finances, how you make decisions, what your values are, and what makes you laugh. They need to hear you admit when you're wrong and see you stand up for your faith. They need to know you inside out—and to feel your interest and belief in them. The word *impart* means "to convey, to contribute, to share fully" ... with children who know without doubt they are "very dear" to you.

C. An unselfish diligence. In verse 9, Paul draws a picture of hard work, of a dad applying himself to the task at hand.

> For you recall, brethren, our labor and hardship, how working night and day so as not to be a burden to any of you, we proclaimed to you the gospel of God.

This is a detailed sketch of financial responsibility and bearing up under the strain of demands. What an example for your children to see! They don't need material goods in place of your time. They don't need to see the fruit of their father's labor instead of their father. But they do need to see their dad do a day's work for a day's pay; and they do need opportunities to earn their own way.

D. A spiritual authenticity. Paul spends verses 9b–10 shading in two important aspects of a father's spiritual responsibility: belief and behavior.

> We proclaimed to you the gospel of God. You are witnesses, and so is God, how devoutly and uprightly and blamelessly we behaved toward you believers.

Too many fathers leave the spiritual aspect of child raising to Mom—if Christ is taught at all, it's usually by the mother. But Paul is showing us that dads need to teach Christ too ... and then live their lives in a way that backs it up.

---

2. Dan Benson, *The Total Man* (Wheaton, Ill.: Tyndale House Publishers, 1977), p. 178.

E. A positive influence. The final stroke on Paul's painting of parenthood is a positive influence.

> Just as you know how we were exhorting and encouraging and imploring each one of you as a father would his own children, so that you may walk in a manner worthy of the God who calls you into His own kingdom and glory. (vv. 11–12)

Dan Benson, in his book *The Total Man,* tells us the results of a disturbing survey: for every single positive statement made in the average home, there are ten negative ones.[3] It's hard to be positive while your kids are maturing. It's part of your job to correct them, right? But children whose ears are full of the words "No" and "Don't" and "Stop that!" learn not to trust their instincts, not to try. Children who hear "That's great!" and "You can do it!" as often as they hear "That's not a good idea" will face new challenges with self-confidence and explore their potential without fear.

"Children Are Wet Cement"

Although cement has certain internal properties that determine how it can be shaped, it nevertheless is greatly influenced by the molding of external forces. In the child's case, that molding influence is the parent. Anne Ortlund illustrates this in her book *Children Are Wet Cement.*

That child of yours is helpless in the hands of the people around him. He is pliable to their shaping; they set his mold. What will he become?

That's what Abraham Lincoln asked—who never paid more than minimum courtesy to the adults whom he passed on the street, but when he passed a child, he stepped out of the way and doffed his hat.

"These adults I know," he said, "but who knows what the children may become?"

These little ones, kicking in their cribs or racing around—they are tomorrow's world, our most precious possession, most powerful potential....

But the awesome thing is that they receive their impressions of life from us—even their impressions of what makes godliness....

---

3. Benson, *The Total Man,* p. 183.

Well, they are God's wonderful gift to us.
Certainly they make us what we would never
be, if they weren't watching us and copying us!
They are the arrows from our bows, with
their direction dependent on our guidance.
They are the receivers of our batons, when
we begin to tire.
They are tomorrow's heroes and rescuers
and achievers—or else tomorrow's thieves and
saboteurs and loafers.[4]

 Living Insights

Study One

1 Thessalonians 2:8–12 shows us a tender picture of a wise dad.
Let's examine the key words in this passage so we can get a better
look at fatherhood from God's perspective.

- What are some of the most meaningful words or phrases in these
five verses? Write them down; then define them, using the context
of the passage and perhaps a Bible dictionary. Finally, explain the
importance of the words and how they add to your understanding
of fatherhood.

Key word/phrase: _____

Definition: _____

_____

Significance: _____

_____

Key word/phrase: _____

Definition: _____

_____

Significance: _____

_____

4. Anne Ortlund, *Children Are Wet Cement* (Old Tappan, N.J.: Fleming H. Revell Co., 1981),
pp. 38–40.

Key word/phrase: _____

Definition: _____

_____

Significance: _____

_____

Key word/phrase: _____

Definition: _____

_____

Significance: _____

_____

Key word/phrase: _____

Definition: _____

_____

Significance: _____

_____

Key word/phrase: _____

Definition: _____

_____

Significance: _____

_____

Key word/phrase: _____

Definition: _____

_____

Significance: _____

_____

Continued on next page

Key word/phrase: _____

Definition: _____

_____

Significance: _____

_____

Key word/phrase: _____

Definition: _____

_____

Significance: _____

_____

Key word/phrase: _____

Definition: _____

_____

Significance: _____

_____

Living Insights

Study Two ━━━━━━━━━━━━━━━━━━━━━━━━━━━━━━

The five qualities discussed in this study are important for all fathers. Dad, how do you measure up in these areas? Use this time to evaluate your effectiveness in fathering by checking (✔) the appropriate box.

A Fond Affection   ☐ Doing Well   ☐ OK   ☐ Needs Work

A Transparent Life   ☐ Doing Well   ☐ OK   ☐ Needs Work

An Unselfish Diligence   ☐ Doing Well   ☐ OK   ☐ Needs Work

A Spiritual Authenticity   ☐ Doing Well   ☐ OK   ☐ Needs Work

A Positive Influence   ☐ Doing Well   ☐ OK   ☐ Needs Work

If this evaluation was affirming, that's great! But if it was more on the convicting side, take heart. Now you have a place to begin. Take one of these areas that may need some work, and do something concrete about it with your children this week.

Mothers:
An Endangered Species
Proverbs 24:3–4, 2 Timothy 1:1–7

She cooks, she cleans, she comforts, she corrects. She has six pairs of hands, and eyes in the back of her head.

Mother. For some, this word conjures up images of June Cleaver, complete with lace apron and pearls—singer of lullabies, baker of brownies, kissing away a child's hot tears. Others envision the Erma Bombeck model, who drives a wood-paneled station wagon and whose hobby is dust. Whatever the type, no one has more influence than a mother. For better or worse, she will forever impact the life of her child.

Tough and tender, wise and warm, a mother must be all things to all her family . . . at all times. That's quite a job description, and anyone who is a mother, or has watched one in action, knows there's no career more demanding. How does she do it? In today's lesson we'll discover the qualities essential to good home building.

I. A Firm Foundation
A. Tools a mother needs.
All homes must be built on a firm foundation. In Proverbs 24:3–4 we see the tools mothers need for establishing a home that is rock-solid.

By wisdom a house is built,
And by understanding it is established;
And by knowledge the rooms are filled
With all precious and pleasant riches.

Solomon is suggesting that homes are built with three primary tools: *wisdom, understanding,* and *knowledge.* Wisdom is the ability to see with discernment, to view life through God's eyes. Understanding is the skill of responding with insight, reading between the lines. Knowledge is the rare trait of going beyond the facts—it's perceiving, discovering, and growing with your child. These tools have nothing to do with hammer and nails or trowel and mortar. They are relational. And mothers, you can have all three. With God-given wisdom, understanding, and knowledge, you can be filling the rooms of your home with a rich heritage of godly character traits, deep relationships, and lasting memories.

┌─ *The Best Translation* ─────────────────────────────
    A story is told of four men arguing over the best translation of the Bible. The first man liked the King James Version because of its beautiful, eloquent English. Another

23

insisted the American Standard Bible was best because of its accuracy to the original text. A third preferred Moffatt for its quaint, penetrating words and captivating phrases. After pondering the issue, the fourth man said, "Personally, I have always preferred my mother's translation." Tolerating the others' chuckles, he responded, "Yes, she translated it. She translated each page of the Bible into life. It is the most convincing translation I ever saw."

B. A New Testament example. The New Testament shows us a mother who used the tools of wisdom, understanding, and knowledge in rearing her son Timothy. Although we don't know much about Timothy's mother, we do know that she and his grandmother made an incredible investment in his spiritual life. So much so that Paul, the wise apostle, was drawn to the young man, forging a fifteen-year friendship with him. As Paul lay dying in a Roman dungeon, Timothy was the friend he sought out.

> Paul, an apostle of Jesus Christ . . . to Timothy, my beloved son. . . . I thank God, whom I serve with a clear conscience the way my forefathers did, as I constantly remember you in my prayers night and day, longing to see you. (2 Tim. 1:1–4a)

Looking back on their friendship, Paul is filled with gratitude and good memories. In the verses that follow, we'll discover the qualities that made Timothy unique and appealing, qualities he learned from his mother.

II. A Mother's Contributions

In verses 4–7 we find five distinct contributions mothers can make to the family, filling each room with her motherly touch until her house becomes a home.

A. Transparent tenderness. Paul first mentions Timothy's tears.

> . . . even as I recall your tears, so that I may be filled with joy. (v. 4)

Paul remembers Timothy's tenderness, a trait passed down from his mother. In fact, most of us learned tenderness from our mothers, while our dads taught us diligence. From Dad we learned the value of a dollar, the significance of honesty, the importance of standing alone when everything turns against us. But we learned transparent tenderness from Mom. Mothers, don't lose that quality—it's one of your greatest contributions to your family. Your warm embrace, eager smile, and soft reply will be a safe harbor for the child who's tossed and battered by life's stormy seas.

B. Authentic spirituality. In verse 5 Paul refers directly to Timothy's heritage, his roots.

> For I am mindful of the sincere faith within you, which first dwelt in your grandmother Lois, and your mother Eunice, and I am sure that it is in you as well.

The Greek term for *sincere* is *anupokritos*, which means "unhypocritical." Nothing phony here; it's real, lived-out faith. Paul knew the sincere faith modeled in Mama Eunice and Grandma Lois had impacted Timothy (see also 3:14–15). That's the way authentic spirituality works. Christian churches, schools, and friends can give children the facts, the words to say. But those words won't fit reality unless God's truth is translated at home.

C. Inner confidence. Paul continues on that theme:

> And for this reason I remind you to kindle afresh the gift of God which is in you through the laying on of my hands. For God has not given us a spirit of timidity, but of *power.* . . . (1:6–7, emphasis added)

In the Greek, *power* has in mind "inherent strength" and "inner might."[1] Notice that timidity is not a desirable trait—it's a synonym for insecurity or inferiority. It's amazing how your children can sense your own attitude toward yourself—and how they will emulate it, good or bad. One of the reasons Timothy stayed true to the Scriptures and stood strong in his ministry was because he had learned inner confidence from his mother.

Made in His Image

Moms, do you know that God wants to use you to build healthy self-esteem in your child? Note these words from family expert Dr. James Dobson:

> It is a wise adult who understands that self-esteem is the most fragile characteristic in human nature, and once broken, its reconstruction is more difficult than repairing Humpty Dumpty. . . .
>
> . . . Although our task is more difficult for some children than for others, there *are* ways to teach a child of his genuine significance, regardless of the shape of his nose or the size of his ears or the efficiency of his mind. *Every* child is entitled to hold up his head, not in haughtiness and pride, but in confidence and security. This is the concept of human worth

---

1. The Greek word is *dunamis,* from which we get our words *dynamic* and *dynamite.*

intended by our Creator. How foolish for us to doubt our value when He formed us in His own image!...

...When the child is convinced that he is greatly loved and respected by his parents, he is inclined to accept his own worth as a person.[2]

Inner confidence, like transparent tenderness and authentic spirituality, is passed down from generation to generation . . . as in Timothy's life, from grandmother to mother to son. How's *your* self-esteem, Mom? Are you taking the time to cultivate a positive self-image in your child?

D. Unselfish love. Let's look again at verse 7 for the fourth contribution mothers make.

For God has not given us a spirit of timidity, but of power and *love*. . . . (emphasis added)

This kind of love—*agapē*—seeks the highest good of the other person. It needs to be evident in every facet of your lives, Moms. And your love shows through in two ways especially. First, in your sense of humor—when you laugh in the midst of pressure and refuse to take yourself too seriously, which gives your child a more positive and unthreatening environment to grow in. And second, in your sense of insight—when you listen to hurts and hear what isn't said, showing your child that you care and want to help.

"The Greatest of These"

In another letter, this time to the Corinthians, Paul devoted an entire chapter to the subject of unselfish love (1 Cor. 13). One mother has written a paraphrase that aptly describes this essential ingredient of mothering.

If I talk to my children about what is right and what is wrong, but have not love, I am like a ringing doorbell or pots banging in the kitchen. And though I know what stages they will go through, and understand their growing pains, and can answer all their questions about life, and believe myself to be a devoted mother, but have not love, I am nothing.

If I give up the fulfillment of a career to make my children's lives better, and stay up all

2. James Dobson, *Hide or Seek*, rev. ed. (Old Tappan, N.J.: Fleming H. Revell Co., 1979), pp. 57, 60, 62. Used by permission.

night sewing costumes or baking cookies on short notice, but grumble about lack of sleep, I have not love and accomplish nothing.

A loving mother is patient with her children's immaturity and kind even when they are not; a loving mother is not jealous of their youth nor does she hold it over their heads whenever she has sacrificed for them. A loving mother does not push her children into doing things her way. She is not irritable, when the chicken pox have kept her confined with three whining children for two weeks, and does not resent the child who brought the affliction home in the first place.

A loving mother is not relieved when her disagreeable child finally disobeys her directly and she can punish him, but rather rejoices with him when he is being more cooperative. A loving mother bears much of the responsibility for her children; she believes in them; she hopes in each one's individual ability to stand out as a light in a dark world; she endures every backache and heartache to accomplish that.

A loving mother never really dies. As for homebaked bread, it will be consumed and forgotten; as for spotless floors, they will soon gather dust and heelmarks. And as for children, well, right now toys, friends, and food are all-important to them. But when they grow up it will have been how their mother loved them that will determine how they love others. In that way she will live on.

So care, training, and a loving mother reside in a home, these three, but the greatest of these is a loving mother.[3]

E. Self-control. Take a final look at 2 Timothy 1:7.

For God has not given us a spirit of timidity, but of power and love and *discipline.* (emphasis added)

Good moms balance tenderness and love with discipline. They set parameters and know when it's time to say "That's it; that's

3. Dianne Lorang, as quoted in *Keep the Fire Glowing,* by Pat Williams, Jill Williams, and Jerry Jenkins (Old Tappan, N.J.: Fleming H. Revell Co., 1986), pp. 152–53.

enough." In his excellent book *Hide or Seek,* James Dobson tells the story of a research project conducted by Dr. Stanley Coopersmith, associate professor of psychology at the University of California. After studying 1,738 middle-class boys and their families over a number of years, Coopersmith identified three important differences between the families of boys with high self-esteem and those with low self-worth. First, *the high-esteem children were more loved and appreciated at home.* Their parents' love was deep and real; their words had substance. Second, and perhaps most revealing, *the high-esteem group had parents whose approach to discipline was significantly more strict.* They taught self-control. In contrast, the parents of the low-esteem group were much more permissive, creating a sense of insecurity. These boys were more likely to feel that no one cared enough to enforce the rules. Third, *the high-esteem group had homes that were characterized by democracy and open communication.* Once boundaries had been established, the boys had the freedom to ask questions and express themselves in an environment of acceptance.[4] Mothers, don't underestimate the value of teaching self-control. In your discipline, you are building your children's character, enhancing their self-esteem, and helping them learn to be responsible for themselves.

Some Points to Ponder

If a child lives with criticism, he learns to condemn.
If a child lives with hostility, he learns to fight.
If a child lives with ridicule, he learns to be shy.
If a child lives with shame, he learns to feel guilty.
If a child lives with tolerance, he learns to be patient.
If a child lives with encouragement, he learns to have confidence.
If a child lives with praise, he learns appreciation.
If a child lives with fairness, he learns justice.
If a child lives with security, he learns to have faith.
If a child lives with approval, he learns to like himself.
If a child lives with acceptance and friendship, he learns to find love in the world.[5]

---

4. Dobson, *Hide or Seek,* pp. 92–93.

5. Dorothy Law Nolte, as quoted in *Children Are Wet Cement,* by Anne Ortlund (Old Tappan, N.J.: Fleming H. Revell Co., 1981), p. 58.

III. A Return to Our Foundation

How do mothers build solid homes? First they secure the foundation. Remember the tools?

> By *wisdom* a house is built,
> And by *understanding* it is established;
> And by *knowledge* the rooms are filled
> With all precious and pleasant riches.
> (Prov. 24:3–4, emphasis added)

And those riches are transparent tenderness, authentic spirituality, inner confidence, unselfish love, and self-control. Children see what God's love is all about through their parents, especially their mothers since they spend the most time with them. Moms, when you laugh, your children hear God laugh. When you cry, they see Him cry. And when you give up your children, letting them go out into the world, they will understand more fully how God gave up His Son. Never doubt the value of your role. Without your positive, supportive partnership, the family could not survive.

 Living Insights

Study One

The apostle Paul writes tenderly in 2 Timothy—his final letter in the Scriptures. Perhaps we can gain some fresh insights into this letter by seeing it in a different light.

- In another version of the New Testament, reread 2 Timothy 1:1–7. You might try the King James, New King James, New American Standard, New International, Revised Standard, or maybe a paraphrase like the Living Bible or The New Testament in Modern English by J. B. Phillips. Remember, the purpose of this exercise is to gain a new perspective on this passage.

Continued on next page

Living Insights

Just as we gave Dad a chance to see how he measured up to some important biblical qualities, we now afford the same opportunity to you, Mom. Evaluate yourself on the qualities we discussed in this lesson by checking (✔) the appropriate box.

Transparent Tenderness   ☐ Doing Well   ☐ OK   ☐ Needs Work

Authentic Spirituality   ☐ Doing Well   ☐ OK   ☐ Needs Work

Inner Confidence   ☐ Doing Well   ☐ OK   ☐ Needs Work

Unselfish Love   ☐ Doing Well   ☐ OK   ☐ Needs Work

Self-control   ☐ Doing Well   ☐ OK   ☐ Needs Work

Let this evaluation be an encouragement to you: let it praise you where praise is due, and let it get you thinking about areas that are less than you'd like them to be. In fact, why not take one of these weaker areas and do something positive about it this week. Who knows, by the end of the week you may surprise yourself, and you'll definitely surprise your children!

Mom and Dad . . .
Meet Your Child
Proverbs 22:6

Most parents view the cooing bundle of baby fat they bring home from the maternity ward as a cuddly lump of clay, soft and totally pliable in their hands. They believe they can take the personality of their baby, squeeze it, roll it, mold it into any shape they desire, pop it into a kiln until it's good and hard, and send it out to face the world.

But that perception of child rearing fails to take into account the properties of the clay itself. Although the clay can be shaped, it can only be shaped to the extent that the properties of the clay allow. And that varies with the type of clay being used. The preestablished characteristics of the clay determine, to a large extent, how it can be shaped and how it will respond to the kiln. So, although the personality of the child can be influenced by the hands of the parent, the preestablished characteristics of the child determine *how* and to what extent it can be molded.

In today's lesson we'll take a look at Proverbs 22:6, a key passage in discovering and developing those characteristics.

> Train up a child in the way he should go,
> Even when he is old he will not depart from it.

As integral as this verse is to raising children, few parents understand what it really says.

I. The Popular Interpretation of Proverbs 22:6
Many see this verse as saying that if children have been carted off to church every Sunday, made to read the Bible each day, instructed to memorize Scripture, taught to read only Christian books and see only Christian films, then those children will stay on the straight and narrow path. And, even if they do play the prodigal and morally journey into some distant country, at some point they will come to their senses and get back on course. As popular as this interpretation is, it doesn't always square with experience. Real life teaches us that not all prodigals come home. The bottom of the ocean is strewn with the wreckage of ships that have strayed from their course and never returned safely to harbor. Sadly, our memories are strewn with the shipwrecked lives of loved ones who charted courses onto the high seas, rode immorality's crest—and sank.

II. The Proper Interpretation of Proverbs 22:6
Not only does the popular interpretation of Proverbs 22:6 not square experientially, it doesn't square exegetically.

31

A. The nature of the training. Let's begin by looking at the words *train up*. The Hebrew term behind this phrase originally referred to the palate or the roof of the mouth.[1] It was used to describe the action of a midwife who, soon after the child's birth, would dip her fingers into the juice of crushed dates and massage the infant's gums and palate. This tangy taste created a sensation for sucking. Then she would place the child in the mother's arms to begin nursing. Likewise, parents are to create a thirst for the nourishing flow of their wisdom and counsel.

B. The duration of the training. The word *child* invariably calls to mind a little one somewhere between infancy and four or five years old. However, the Scriptures use the term in a broader sense, ranging anywhere from a newborn to a person of marriageable age.[2] The point is that the principle applies to any dependent child still living under the parents' roof.

C. The implementation of the training. The manner of training is suggested by the word *in,* which means "in keeping with, in cooperation with, in accordance to something." The literal rendering is "according to his way." That's altogether different from *your* way, *your* plan, *your* curriculum. The verse doesn't mean "Train up a child as you see him." Rather, "If you want your training to be meaningful and wise, be observant and discover your child's way, and adapt your training accordingly." Strengthening this idea is the word *way.*[3] Notice its use in Proverbs 30:18–19.

> There are three things which are too wonderful for me,
> Four which I do not understand:
> The way of an eagle in the sky,
> The way of a serpent on a rock,
> The way of a ship in the middle of the sea,
> And the way of a man with a maid.

The Hebrew term for *way* literally means "road" or "path." In a figurative sense, it means a "characteristic." In Proverbs 22:6, the underlying idea is that the child's characteristics are pre-formed by God, distinct and set. The word *bent* describes the

---

1. The word was also used for breaking a wild horse by placing a rope in its mouth, thereby bringing it into submission.

2. Although translated differently at times, the same Hebrew word for *child* is used in many different passages. For example, in 1 Samuel 4:21 the term *boy* is used of a newborn infant. In Exodus 2:2–3 *child* is used to describe three-month-old Moses. In 1 Samuel 1:22 it is used of Samuel before he was weaned. In Genesis 21:12–20 *lad* is used to refer to Ishmael, a preteen. In Genesis 37:2 *youth* is used of Joseph at age 17. And in Genesis 34:19 *young man* is used of a boy of marriageable age.

3. In Hebrew the noun form is *derek;* the verb form is *darak.*

infant's personality perfectly.[4] Each child is not a totally pliable lump of clay but has certain bents prescribed according to a predetermined pattern. And these bents greatly affect how the child should be handled and how moldable the child will be.

"Fearfully and Wonderfully Made"

Each child is hand-stitched by the Lord—not mass-manufactured in some sweatshop. The mind is intricately woven with the finest of neurological threads. The emotions are given a distinct texture, with a feel all their own. The personality is cut from a unique bolt of cloth. Like snowflakes and fingerprints, no two are alike.

Consider the radical differences in these Old Testament brothers: Cain and Abel . . . Solomon and Absalom . . . even Jacob and Esau, who were twins, demonstrated significant physical and psychological differences.

Now consider your children. How different each is. How distinct—physically, mentally, emotionally, spiritually. God wants you to know your children, to appreciate the unique way they were crafted, and to train them according to their specific characteristics.

As parents, we must be careful to avoid two errors: first, rearing our children the way we were reared—mistakes and all; and second, comparing our children with each other and applying the same approach to all. Both errors stem from a failure to understand and appreciate how fearfully and wonderfully each was made.

D. **The results of the training.** The latter portion of Proverbs 22:6 states that "when he is old he will not depart from it." The root meaning of the Hebrew word for *old* is "hair on the chin." It suggests someone approaching adulthood, not approaching retirement. Solomon is not envisioning a ninety-year-old prodigal returning home. He's thinking of a boy who's just starting to grow a beard. Thus, when the child reaches maturity, he will not depart from the way in which he has been trained.

III. The Parental Application of Proverbs 22:6

Two questions arise for the parent intent on applying this passage of Scripture: How can I know my child's bents? and, What are those

---

4. The basic concept behind the verb *darak* has to do with setting foot on territory or objects. In Psalm 7:12 the word is used of God who "has bent His bow and made it ready." That is, He has set His foot on the bow in order to bend it and string it. In a similar way, God puts His foot on the physical, psychological, and personality bows of our lives to bend them in specific ways.

bents, so I can nurture them? We'll answer the first question now and the second one in the next lesson. If we look closely at Proverbs 20:11–13, the answer to the first question will come into focus.

It is by his deeds that a lad distinguishes himself
If his conduct is pure and right.
The hearing ear and the seeing eye,
The Lord has made both of them.
Do not love sleep, lest you become poor;
Open your eyes, and you will be satisfied with food.

This passage tells us we are to observe our children and *how* we are to observe them—with diligence. We shouldn't let our eyes droop or sleep. We must be awake and alert to how our children respond to life situations. Basically that takes two things—time and concentration. Your children *are* making themselves known. The question is, are you noticing? If you're beginning to feel that you don't really know or understand them, now is the best time to start. You don't need a degree in theology . . . or a Ph.D. in psychology . . . or even an uncommon portion of common sense. All you need is a sensitive spirit. And you can start right now, simply by asking God to begin making you more sensitive to the unique qualities He created in your children.

 ## Living Insights

Study One ━━━━━━━━━━━━━━━━━━━━━━━━━━━━━━

For this study we want to participate in a fairly simple exercise. But don't let its simplicity fool you. It's a vital part of internalizing the Word of God.

- Memorize Proverbs 22:6. Write the verse down on a note card, and begin repeating it aloud. In a short time you'll know the verse by heart.

 ## Living Insights

Study Two ━━━━━━━━━━━━━━━━━━━━━━━━━━━━━━

Before we journey on to discover the bents in our children, it would be extremely valuable to discover the bents in ourselves.

- What's your personality like? Have you ever given it much thought? Use the space that follows to write down your observations. This exercise could be a time to discover some exciting things about yourself.

My Bents

Physically

_____

_____

_____

_____

Mentally

_____

_____

_____

_____

Emotionally

_____

_____

_____

_____

Spiritually

_____

_____

_____

_____

The Bents in Your Baby

Proverbs 22:6, Psalm 139

Raising children is a lot like baking a cake. If you follow the wrong recipe, you won't realize it until it's too late!

In baking, it is essential to use the proper ingredients in the proper amounts. Yet in a busy kitchen, it's easy to skim over the directions and confuse a tablespoon with a teaspoon or baking soda with baking powder. It's easy, too, in the interest of economy, to make a few compromises. To substitute margarine for butter. Or imitation vanilla for the real thing.

But too many compromises and too many miscalculations could leave you with a mess on your hands—both in the kitchen and in your children's lives.

Today we'll review a recipe Proverbs 22:6 gives for raising a child. Then we'll take a look at a few more ingredients from the bountiful cupboards of the Psalms.

I. Review of Foundational Information

Proverbs 22:6 implies that we need to *know* our child, to familiarize ourselves with the distinct ingredients God has placed within that little package of a person. This is the primary task of parenting.

Train up a child in the way he should go,
Even when he is old he will not depart from it.

We might paraphrase the verse to read: "Adapt the training of your children so that it is in keeping with their individual gifts or *bents*— the God-given characteristics built into them at birth. When maturity comes, they will not leave the training they have received." Two significant observations arise from this verse.

A. A child's characteristics are built in. A child is not a soft lump of dough that we can shape into anything we want if we just exert enough pressure. On the contrary, each child is deposited into our arms as a package of pre-sifted, premeasured ingredients—ingredients that determine whether the child will turn out as a cake or a loaf of bread. This leads us to a second observation.

B. Parental sensitivity to those characteristics is vital. Discovering those ingredients is the most essential task of parenting. This requires a great deal of sensitivity. Proverbs 20:11a says that a child's character will make itself known by its actions. Yet parents must be diligent in observing their children in order to cooperate with the right bents and correct the wrong

36

bents in their character (vv. 12–13). Parenting requires enormous amounts of patience, time, energy, and concentration. And unless the parent gets actively involved in the process, the child's whole future will be impaired.

The rod and reproof give wisdom,
But a child who gets his own way brings shame to
his mother. (29:15)

Literally, the latter half of the verse means, "a child *left to himself* brings shame to his mother." Passive parenting is like passive farming. Without diligent cultivation, we can expect little more than a harvest of weeds.

II. Knowledge of Internal Bents

All this raises two very practical questions: What are my child's bents? and, How can I nurture them? These internal characteristics are not spelled out in Scripture, but we are given some guidelines as to what they might include. In every child there are bents toward good as well as evil. Let's look first at Psalm 139 to examine the good bents; then we'll go to Psalm 58 to examine the bad.

A. Toward good.

  1. **Generally.** Psalm 139 is one of the most magnificent of all the ancient hymns. It revolves around God: His knowledge of all things (vv. 1–6), His presence in all places (vv. 7–12), His power over all things (vv. 13–16), and His redemptive scrutiny (vv. 23–24). Notice how David describes God's intimate knowledge of his life.

O Lord, Thou hast searched me and known me.
Thou dost know when I sit down and when I rise
up;
Thou dost understand my thought from afar.
Thou dost scrutinize my path and my lying down,
And art intimately acquainted with all my ways.
(vv. 1–3)

God knows us long before our parents do. And His knowledge is not superficial, but it searches to the depths of our being. He knows all our bents, even the most intricate. How could that be? Because He works in the darkness of a tiny womb, delicately embroidering His *magnum opus,* the most regal of all His creative work—a human being.

For Thou didst form my inward parts;
Thou didst weave me in my mother's womb.
(v. 13)

Like a fiber-optic camera exploring the womb, the Creator takes us on a guided tour of the developing fetus.[1] The word *Thou* in verse 13 is placed first in the Hebrew sentence to emphasize its importance: "Thou" and none other—not Mother Nature, not chance, not fate—"didst form my inward parts." The verb *form* means "originated or created." And *inward parts* is literally "kidneys," which the Hebrews used to represent the vital organs, including the lungs, heart, brain, and liver. The image in the second part of verse 13 conveys the idea of knitting something together. With that embryonic ball of yarn, God knits together each child. It is no small wonder that David bursts into praise in verse 14.

I will give thanks to Thee, for I am fearfully and
 wonderfully made;
Wonderful are Thy works,
And my soul knows it very well.

David continues the anatomy lesson in verse 15.

My frame was not hidden from Thee,
When I was made in secret,
And skillfully wrought in the depths of the earth.

The word *frame* means "bony substance," another way of saying skeleton.[2] The term *skillfully wrought* has a beautiful Hebrew meaning, which can be seen in Exodus where the Tabernacle curtains are described. They were variegated, like a multicolored tapestry, and embroidered like fine needlepoint. The next phrase speaks of "the depths of the earth." This is a poetic way of describing the womb by comparing it to the darkened caverns below the earth's surface. Seen as such, the womb is a place of concealment and protection. Continuing, David shows that God plans our lives, which He so diligently fashions in the cover of darkness.

---

1. Some stunning examples of fiber-optic photography that display life developing within the womb and illustrate Psalm 139 can be found in the book *A Child Is Born,* by Lennart Nilsson (New York, N.Y.: Delacorte Press, 1977).

2. In the fascinating book *Fearfully and Wonderfully Made,* the surgeon who coauthored the book wrote these words about our frame: "In comparison [to bone], wood can withstand even less pulling tension, and could not possibly bear the compression forces that bone can. A wooden pole for the vaulter would quickly snap. Steel, which can absorb both forces well, is three times the weight of bone and would burden us down. The economical body takes this stress-bearing bone and hollows it out, using a weight-saving architectural principle it took people millennia to discover; it then fills the vacant space in the center with an efficient red blood cell factory that turns out a trillion new cells per day. Bone sheathes life." Dr. Paul Brand and Philip Yancey, *Fearfully and Wonderfully Made* (Grand Rapids, Mich.: Zondervan Publishing House, 1980), p. 70.

Thine eyes have seen my unformed substance;
And in Thy book they were all written,
The days that were ordained for me,
When as yet there was not one of them.
(Ps. 139:16)

Unformed substance is used in the Talmud to indicate every kind of unshapen material, like a block of wood or a lump of clay. When applied to a human vessel, it would be equivalent to the embryo.

Building from God's Blueprints

"Thine eyes have seen my unformed substance" means something far more than God sitting in the grandstands and spectating while the child develops. The word *seen* means "watched over." It is used in an active sense, like architects who painstakingly watch over every detail of construction to make sure the builders adhere to their blueprints. The bents in a child's blueprint—at least the good ones—are designed by God, and He oversees their placement during the gestation period. So much so that even the very days of the child are delineated.

Are you watching over your children to discover their bents with the same diligence that God took in His design? Are you studying the architecture of their physical and psychological makeup, looking for God's blueprint and appreciating each strategically placed detail in their personality? Or have you ignored the existing structure and begun a building project of your own, with your own blueprints in mind?

The psalmist wants you to realize that the sovereign architect of heaven has given you a sacred and unique edifice. He has given that special child to you for only a limited time. Make the most of that time, won't you? Get started on the right foundation, and get to know the child God has so graciously entrusted to your custodial care.

---

2. **Specifically.** Now that we have seen the tremendous care God has taken in making our children unique, how do we go about discovering and nurturing the good bents He's placed in these little works of art? What are some things to look for? Since we are created in His image and likeness

39

(Gen. 1:26–27), we are endowed with such traits as intelligence, creativity, a desire to love and be loved, imagination, memory, and feelings. He's also given each of us certain talents, gifts, and aptitudes. And, because we are the work of His hands, we have a built-in longing for Him . . . a spiritual bent. All of these are gifts from God, preformed by Him, and shaped differently to create the uniqueness of each child.

Unwrapping God's Gifts

In his poem, "The Completeness of This Child," Ulrich Schaffer expresses feelings similar to David's awe of God's craftsmanship.

i am amazed
at the completeness of this child
nothing is missing
this is a person like i am

there is a richness of emotion
a struggling with the will
a facing of anxiety
abandonment in joy
a life full of hope and failure
of disappointment and joy
a life not different from my own . . .

i have to take more seriously
each phase of growth
and learn to live inside the head
that feels and doubts and questions[3]

Let's learn to study our children in order to nurture their good bents. Because to miss them is like getting a beautiful present from God . . . and never bothering to unwrap it.

B. Toward evil. Coined in the image of God, the child bears a certain imprint of divinity. But that coin also bears the defacing effects of the Fall. Like Midas in reverse, Adam's touch on us all has turned the luster of God's image into tarnish (Rom. 5:12). Psalm 51:5 underscores this bent toward evil.

Behold, I was brought forth in iniquity,
And in sin my mother conceived me.

---

3. Excerpt from "The Completeness of This Child," from *For the Love of Children,* by Ulrich Schaffer. © 1980 by Ulrich Schaffer. Reprinted by permission of Harper and Row, Publishers, Inc.

David is not saying that the act of conception is evil, but that at the time of birth he possessed a sinful nature. Psalm 58:2–5 expounds on this idea.

No, in heart you work unrighteousness;
On earth you weigh out the violence of your hands.
The wicked are estranged from the womb;
These who speak lies go astray from birth.
They have venom like the venom of a serpent;
Like a deaf cobra that stops up its ear,
So that it does not hear the voice of charmers,
Or a skillful caster of spells.

Note the fateful words *from the womb*. From the very inception of life, sin is inbred into human nature. Like a serpent, our nature is full of deadly poison. And like a cobra, it is deaf to reproof. No matter how cute and cuddly that little baby is in your arms, it is not free from sin—childhood innocence shouldn't be confused with moral purity. The Adamic bent is vividly illustrated in the history of humankind and even more clearly set forth in Scripture.

"There is none righteous, not even one;
There is none who understands,
There is none who seeks for God;
All have turned aside, together they have become
    useless;
There is none who does good,
There is not even one."
"Their throat is an open grave,
With their tongues they keep deceiving,"
"The poison of asps is under their lips."
(Rom. 3:10b–13)

The only antidote to sin's poison is counteraction, on both a divine and a human level. Divine help is needed to bring the child to a saving knowledge of Christ; human help is needed to discipline the child. Remember Proverbs 29:15?

The rod and reproof give wisdom,
But a child who gets his own way brings shame to
his mother.

Like Begets Like

Just as physical characteristics are hereditary, so the personal characteristics of the parents are passed down generation after generation. Two contrasting cases in point are worthy of our attention:

"The father of Jonathan Edwards was a minister and his mother was the daughter of a clergyman. Among their descendants were fourteen presidents of colleges, more than one hundred college professors, more than one hundred lawyers, thirty judges, sixty physicians, more than a hundred clergymen, missionaries and theology professors, and about sixty authors. There is scarcely any great American industry that has not had one of his family among its chief promoters. Such is the product of one American Christian family, reared under the most favorable conditions. The contrast is presented in the Jukes family, which could not be made to study and would not work, and is said to have cost the state of New York a million dollars. Their entire record is one of pauperism and crime, insanity and imbecility. Among their twelve hundred known descendants, three hundred ten were professional paupers, four hundred forty were physically wrecked by their own wickedness, sixty were habitual thieves, one hundred thirty were convicted criminals, fifty-five were victims of impurity, only twenty learned a trade (and ten of these learned it in a state prison), and this notorious family produced seven murderers."[4]

What qualities and character traits are you passing down to your children? Are you actively involved in knowing your children, guiding them toward maturity? Or are you passively allowing their evil bents to run rampant? Remember, the legacy you leave will shape your family for generations to come.

 Living Insights

Study One

Psalm 139 is a lyrical masterpiece. It revolves around God's presence, power, and redemptive scrutiny. Let's take a closer look at this beautiful psalm.

---

4. As quoted by J. Oswald Sanders, in *A Spiritual Clinic* (Chicago, Ill.: Moody Press, 1958), p. 90.

- Psalm 139 can be divided into six stanzas, with each section looking at God from a different angle. In this exercise, study the psalm stanza by stanza. Try to find out what each section is teaching you about God, yourself, and your child.

Psalm 139

Stanza 1 (vv. 1–6) _____

_____

_____

_____

_____

_____

_____

Stanza 2 (vv. 7–12) _____

_____

_____

_____

_____

_____

_____

Stanza 3 (vv. 13–16) _____

_____

_____

_____

Continued on next page

_____

_____

_____

_____

Stanza 4 (vv. 17–18) _____

_____

_____

_____

_____

_____

Stanza 5 (vv. 19–22) _____

_____

_____

_____

_____

_____

_____

Stanza 6 (vv. 23–24) _____

_____

_____

_____

_____

Living Insights

A study like this one helps us learn why our children are the way they are. Mom or Dad, it's time to take a detailed look at the bents in your baby.

● Map out the bents in your child just as you did for yourself in the last lesson. If you have more than one child, make sure you take the time to write about the bents in each son or daughter.

My Child's Bents

Physically

_____

_____

_____

_____

Mentally

_____

_____

_____

_____

Emotionally

_____

_____

_____

_____

Spiritually

_____

_____

_____

_____

A Chip off the Old Bent
Exodus 34:5–8

Physicians tell us that deformities are often hereditary, as are certain diseases and predispositions to disease. Psychiatrists state that mental illnesses and emotional problems are also sometimes inherited. It stands to reason, then, that certain spiritual characteristics may also be passed down from generation to generation.

Regarding spiritual genetics, our heritage contains three major aspects. One, every person is born in the image of God, with a God-given personality and distinct abilities (Gen. 1:26–27). Two, every person is born with a sin nature, a general bent toward evil inherited from Adam (Rom. 5:12). And three, each of us has a *specific* bent or tendency toward evil inherited from our immediate forefathers. It is this third area that we're going to investigate in our lesson today.

I. Evil Bent Defined and Explained
According to Scripture, all humans are born estranged from God (Ps. 51:5, 58:3; Rom. 3:10–18; Eph. 2:3; Col. 1:21).
A. Generally—from Adam.
When Adam sinned in the Garden of Eden, he was acting as the representative of all humankind.

> Therefore, just as through one man sin entered into the world, and death through sin, and so death spread to all men, because all sinned. (Rom. 5:12)

We can trace the root of our evil bent back to the first man. But the fruit of that bent—the evil thoughts, words, and actions themselves—can be traced more immediately to the branches of our own family tree.
B. Specifically—from Mom and Dad.
Think about yourself for a minute. Chances are, if you take a good look in the mirror, you'll see a striking reflection of the weaknesses you saw in your parents. The resemblance may be a violent temper, deception, sexual weakness, or anxiety. If the characteristic was a dominant gene in your parents' spiritual chemistry, you can count on it being passed down to you.

II. Biblical Basis for Specific Bents toward Evil
By precept and example the Bible demonstrates how specific bents toward evil branch out from each family tree.
A. Actual iniquity is transferred.
In Exodus 34:5–8, amid the clefts of Mount Sinai, Moses brushes with God's glory in an awesome daybreak encounter.

> And the Lord descended in the cloud and stood there with him as he called upon the name of the Lord. Then the Lord passed by in front of him and proclaimed,

"The Lord, the Lord God, compassionate and gracious, slow to anger, and abounding in lovingkindness and truth; who keeps lovingkindness for thousands, who forgives iniquity, transgression and sin; yet He will by no means leave the guilty unpunished, visiting the iniquity of fathers on the children and on the grandchildren to the third and fourth generations." And Moses made haste to bow low toward the earth and worship.

Glinting in the morning sun, the foreboding edge of God's revelation catches our eye: "Visiting the iniquity of fathers on the children and on the grandchildren to the third and fourth generations" (v. 7b). The term *iniquity* is from a Hebrew word meaning "to bend, to twist, to distort, to pervert." In Proverbs 12:8 the term is translated "perverse." At first glance this seems vengeful and unfair. Yet God could have allowed that same perversion or bent to continue throughout the family's history, fraying the entire family line. But God says "No—it will have rippling effects *only* to the third and fourth generations."[1] The scales, then, are weighted not on God's harshness but on His kindness, demonstrating that He is indeed compassionate, gracious, and abounding in lovingkindness for thousands.

B. **Families transmit similar character traits.** The books of Kings and Chronicles document the civil war that split the nation of Israel into two kingdoms. The southern kingdom was ruled by Solomon's son Rehoboam. The reins to the northern kingdom, however, were given to the wicked Jeroboam, Solomon's trusted servant, who spurred the nation on to runaway sinfulness. Twenty-one times in Kings and Chronicles we read that the nation "walked in the way of Jeroboam" (see 1 Kings 15:34, 16:26). Jeroboam's descendants inherited his sins of idolatry, immorality, and rebellion. Like three thorny vines, these bents grew out from Jeroboam and inextricably entangled themselves in the nation—until, at last, God had to brandish the pruning shears of judgment.

C. **A case study: Abraham's family.** Turning back the pages of Israel's history, we'll follow a specific bent—deception—through four generations.

---

1. "But when, on the other hand, the hating ceases, when the children forsake their fathers' evil ways, the warmth of the divine wrath is turned into the warmth of love ... and this mercy endures not only to the third and fourth generation, but to the thousandth generation, though only in relation to those who love God, and manifest this love by keeping His commandments." C. F. Keil and F. Delitzsch, *Commentary on the Old Testament* (Grand Rapids, Mich.: William B. Eerdmans Publishing Co., n.d.), vol. 1, pp. 117–18.

1. **Abraham.** Abraham's propensity to shade the truth is brought to light in Genesis 12.

> Now there was a famine in the land; so Abram went down to Egypt to sojourn there, for the famine was severe in the land. And it came about when he came near to Egypt, that he said to Sarai his wife, "See now, I know that you are a beautiful woman; and it will come about when the Egyptians see you, that they will say, 'This is his wife'; and they will kill me, but they will let you live. Please say that you are my sister so that it may go well with me because of you, and that I may live on account of you." (vv. 10–13)

The truth was that Sarah was Abraham's *half* sister. But he shaded that part of the truth. Looking further at Abraham's life, we see that this tendency to lie—a well-established bent in his character—crops up again. Look at a similar incident in Genesis 20.

> Now Abraham journeyed from there toward the land of the Negev, and settled between Kadesh and Shur; then he sojourned in Gerar. And Abraham said of Sarah his wife, "She is my sister." So Abimelech king of Gerar sent and took Sarah. But God came to Abimelech in a dream of the night, and said to him, "Behold, you are a dead man because of the woman whom you have taken, for she is married." Now Abimelech had not come near her; and he said, "Lord, wilt Thou slay a nation, even though blameless? Did he not himself say to me, 'She is my sister'? And she herself said, 'He is my brother.' " ... And Abimelech said to Abraham, "What have you encountered, that you have done this thing?" And Abraham said, "Because I thought, surely there is no fear of God in this place; and they will kill me because of my wife. Besides, she actually is my sister, the daughter of my father, but not the daughter of my mother, and she became my wife; and it came about, when God caused me to wander from my father's house, that I said to her, 'This is the kindness which you will show to me: everywhere we go, say of me, "He is my brother." ' " (vv. 1–5a, 10–13)

Abraham reasoned that since Sarah was his father's daughter from another marriage, and therefore technically his half sister, he was speaking the truth. The only flaw in that line of reasoning is that he implied something entirely false—that she was *only* a sister.

2. **Isaac.** As Abraham's family tree spreads its branches, we see the seeds of this trait crop up in the second generation. The bent of lying sprouts in Isaac's life through a situation similar to the one his father had experienced years earlier.

> So Isaac lived in Gerar. When the men of the place asked about his wife, he said, "She is my sister," for he was afraid to say, "my wife," thinking, "the men of the place might kill me on account of Rebekah, for she is beautiful." And it came about, when he had been there a long time, that Abimelech king of the Philistines looked out through a window, and saw, and behold, Isaac was caressing his wife Rebekah. Then Abimelech called Isaac and said, "Behold, certainly she is your wife! How then did you say, 'She is my sister'?" And Isaac said to him, "Because I said, 'Lest I die on account of her.'" And Abimelech said, "What is this you have done to us? One of the people might easily have lain with your wife, and you would have brought guilt upon us." (26:6–10)

The same crooked bent from Abraham's life resurfaced in the life of Isaac. We can't help but think, "Like father, like son."

3. **Jacob.** From there, because unchecked, this flaw was passed from Isaac to his son Jacob. Isaac and Rebekah had twin sons, Jacob and Esau, with bents that went in different directions. At an early age Jacob began to develop a Machiavellian habit of doing whatever he needed to gain the advantage, no matter how manipulative or mercenary (see 25:27–33). Encouraged by his mother, his habit culminated in a treacherous act of deception. Jacob deceived his father Isaac into giving him a greater blessing than his brother. Notice how one lie was placed upon another, lending authenticity to his masquerade.

> Then Rebekah took the best garments of Esau her elder son, which were with her in the house, and put them on Jacob her younger son. And she put the skins of the kids on his hands and on the

smooth part of his neck. She also gave the savory food and the bread, which she had made, to her son Jacob. Then he came to his father and said, "My father." And he said, "Here I am. Who are you, my son?" And Jacob said to his father, "I am Esau your firstborn; I have done as you told me. Get up, please, sit and eat of my game, that you may bless me." And Isaac said to his son, "How is it that you have it so quickly, my son?" And he said, "Because the Lord your God caused it to happen to me." Then Isaac said to Jacob, "Please come close, that I may feel you, my son, whether you are really my son Esau or not." So Jacob came close to Isaac his father, and he felt him and said, "The voice is the voice of Jacob, but the hands are the hands of Esau." And he did not recognize him, because his hands were hairy like his brother Esau's hands; so he blessed him. And he said, "Are you really my son Esau?" And he said, "I am." So he said, "Bring it to me, and I will eat of my son's game, that I may bless you." And he brought it to him, and he ate; he also brought him wine and he drank. Then his father Isaac said to him, "Please come close and kiss me, my son." So he came close and kissed him; and when he smelled the smell of his garments, he blessed him. (27:15–27a)

So entrenched was this habit that even when Jacob was old, deception continued to persist in his life (see 43:2–6).

4. **The sons of Jacob.** Tragically, Jacob's habit of deception became so ingrained that it left an imprint in the lives of his twelve sons. Like his parents, Jacob also had his favorites, the foremost being Joseph. But the other sons resented this. And in a jealous dispute over the interpretation of a dream Joseph had, the other brothers sold him to a slave caravan (chap. 37). To cover the crime, the brothers took Joseph's distinctive, multicolored coat, dipped it in animal's blood, and brought it to their father, explaining, "We found this; please examine it to see whether it is your son's tunic or not" (v. 32). That was the spoken lie. They hadn't found it. The whole scene, props and all, was staged. The second lie was unspoken.

Then he examined it and said, "It is my son's tunic. A wild beast has devoured him; Joseph has surely been torn to pieces!" (v. 33)

50

Jacob went into mourning, and his sons did not say a word. In fact, they comforted him. By their silence, they lied. Like father, like sons.

III. Some Suggestions to Sincere Yet Struggling Parents
A lesson like this can be depressing, particularly when we see the skeletons of our own character flaws fleshed out in our children. As genuinely concerned parents, how can we keep from passing on those destructive bents? Here are four suggestions.

  A. Lead your child to faith in Christ. The first and biggest step in straightening out the bents is for your child to become aligned with Him who is "the way, and the truth, and the life" (John 14:6). The Holy Spirit makes that alignment possible because He works internally to create a pliable spirit.

  B. Ask for God's wisdom in studying your child. Observe your child's words (Luke 6:45) and actions (1 Tim. 5:25), because they reflect character ... or the lack of it.

  C. As you set limits, be fair and consistent. Consistency is what shapes character over the long haul. It gives your children the security they need to entrust themselves to your hands.

  D. Do everything in your power to maintain open and loving communication with your child. You will never know your child unless you take control of your schedule and plan time just to listen and observe. This may require putting the TV to bed early instead of the children. Or how about taking your child to work one day instead of bringing your work home? Whatever it takes, your child is worth it!

 Living Insights

Study One ▬▬▬▬▬▬▬▬▬▬▬▬▬▬▬▬▬▬▬▬▬▬▬▬

"Like father, like son." As we saw in our lesson, Abraham's bent toward lying was not isolated in his life alone, but it spread like a cancer through three generations after him. Mom and Dad, how are you doing at cancer prevention? Let's use this time to take an X ray of the flaws that may be plaguing your family, and then apply the sharp scalpel of Scripture to eradicate this disease.

● In the left column of the following chart, write down some less than desirable traits you've seen in your parents, yourself, and now your children. Then, with the help of a concordance, list what the Bible has to say about these bents. Prayerfully consider what God is telling you through His Word.

Cancer Prevention	
Family Trait	God's Remedy

Living Insights

Combating these destructive bents in yourself is hard enough, but when you have to face them in your children, these bents are enough to give a struggling parent the bends! Let's see if we can get straightened out by evaluating ourselves in light of the four concluding points of this lesson.

Unbending the Bents			
Four Concluding Points	Doing Great	Needs Work	Flop City
Lead your child to faith in Christ.	☐	☐	☐
Ask for God's wisdom in studying your child.	☐	☐	☐
As you set limits, be fair and consistent.	☐	☐	☐
Do everything in your power to maintain open and loving communication with your child.	☐	☐	☐

● How are you doing in these areas? Do some of these need work? Do you find yourself in the suburbs of "Flop City"? If so, use the rest of the Living Insights time to plan a strategy for improving one of these weaker areas.

The area I'll begin working on: _____

_____

_____

The strategy I'll be implementing: _____

_____

_____

_____

_____

_____

_____

When Brothers and Sisters Battle
Selected Scripture

In his book *The Strong-Willed Child,* Dr. James Dobson comments on the scourge of sibling rivalry:

> If American women were asked to indicate *the* most irritating feature of child rearing, I'm convinced that sibling rivalry would get their unanimous vote. Little children (and older ones too) are not content just to hate each other in private. They attack one another like miniature warriors, mobilizing their troops and probing for a weakness in the defensive line. They argue, hit, kick, scream, grab toys, taunt, tattle, and sabotage the opposing forces.[1]

If your home is a war zone of sibling rivalry and you often find yourself in a foxhole waving a little white flag, this lesson could deploy the reinforcements you need to survive the battle.

I. Sibling Rivalry: The Biblical Record

The earliest record of a family feud is in the fourth chapter of Genesis, a grisly reminder of the aftereffects of the Fall (vv. 1–8). Before the Fall, the first man and woman bore God's likeness.

> This is the book of the generations of Adam. In the day when God created man, He made him *in the likeness of God.* (5:1, emphasis added)

But after the Fall, that pristine image was defaced. From then on, the image was no longer exclusively God's, but man's; it would bear the craggy features of sin.

> When Adam had lived one hundred and thirty years, he became the father of a son *in his own likeness,* according to his image, and named him Seth. (v. 3, emphasis added)

A. Several examples. As we forage our way through Genesis, we can easily glean from its furrowed chapters several examples of sibling rivalry.

   1. Cain and Abel. By the time Adam's boys reached maturity, sibling rivalry was already deeply rooted—one garden which Adam obviously tended with a negligent hand. In fact, the rivalry became so severe that it came to a bloody resolution one day when Cain killed his brother in the field (4:8–15).[2]

---

1. James Dobson, *The Strong-Willed Child* (Wheaton, Ill.: Tyndale House Publishers, 1978), p. 126. Used by permission.

2. The Hebrew in verse 8 literally says that Cain *slit the throat* of his brother.

2. **Jacob and Esau.** In the home of Isaac and Rebekah, parental loyalties were divided right down the middle of the house. Isaac pulled at Esau; Rebekah tugged at Jacob. And it eventually tore the family apart (25:28). Although Esau was the rightful heir to the lion's share of his father's estate, his mother was partial to Jacob. Her favoritism led her to conspire with Jacob to deceive the patriarch into conferring his blessing upon Jacob rather than Esau (27:1–27). This set fire to the coals of Esau's anger, which had been smoldering for years over unresolved conflict with his brother (v. 36). In his burning rage, he plotted to kill Jacob when their father died (v. 41).

3. **Jacob's sons.** Joseph was the favored son in Jacob's family. All the brothers knew it—and resented it. So severe was this war of sibling rivalry that they plotted to kill Joseph (37:18). But given a cool moment to reconsider, his hotheaded brothers sold Joseph into slavery instead, quenching the embers of hate that glowed in their hearts (v. 28).

B. **Three observations.** In each of the stories we've studied, hatred blazed so intensely that murderous thoughts inflamed hearts and singed consciences. Three observations emerge from what we've seen thus far. One, *no family is immune to sibling rivalry.* The homes we've looked into are some of the most prominent in the Old Testament. Two, *no family problem is unique.* Sibling rivalry weaves a stubborn thread through the centuries. And three, *no solution is easy.*

II. A Special Case Study: David's Family

David. A man after God's own heart. Giant-killer. King. Songwriter. Warrior. He was idolized by generations . . . but, as we will see, this idol had feet of clay. For although he was successful on the throne, he was a failure at home.

A. **General atmosphere of the home.** Before we put a halo around David's head and a harp in his hand, let's take a good look at his home. David ascended to the throne when he was thirty years old and reigned for forty years (2 Sam. 5:4–5). No longer was he an obscure shepherd boy. He was now the single most important person in Israel. No longer was he surrounded by obstinate sheep, but by obsequious servants who responded to his slightest wish. No longer did he spend the night on the hard ground under the stars, but in the plush splendor of the palace. Times had changed. And so had David. The king had become preoccupied with the throne. From breakfast until bedtime he was faced with one decision after another. He became

55

obsessed. And one of those obsessions involved women, which 2 Samuel 5:13 makes note of.

> Meanwhile David took more concubines and wives from Jerusalem, after he came from Hebron; and more sons and daughters were born to David.[3]

In all, David had at least eight wives, which resulted in twenty sons[4] and a daughter.[5] Add his concubines to that number, and you have the full-blown cast for a prime-time soap opera. Think of the jealousy that must have existed between the wives and concubines—not to mention between the children. Whatever problems you have at home, David had them compounded with interest! Hardly the home in which to raise healthy, happy children.

B. Specific conflicts between the children. As time passed and the children of this tangled family grew, you can imagine the knotty circumstances that came up and the frayed feelings that resulted from family feuds (see chaps. 13–18).[6]

1. **A brother disgraces his sister.** Second Samuel 13:1–14 records the shameful rape of Tamar by Amnon, her half brother.

   > He took hold of her and said to her, "Come, lie with me, my sister." But she answered him, "No, my brother, do not violate me, for such a thing is not done in Israel; do not do this disgraceful thing! . . ." However, he would not listen to her; since he was stronger than she, he violated her and lay with her. (vv. 11b–12, 14)

2. **Hatred festers between half brothers.** Even though Tamar's loyal brother Absalom urged her to sweep the scandal under the rug, he couldn't sweep it from his heart.

   > But Absalom did not speak to Amnon either good or bad; for Absalom hated Amnon because he had violated his sister Tamar. (v. 22)

3. **Absalom murders Amnon.** In the absence of a father who would mediate family tensions, hostility simmered in the

---

3. According to Scripture, David had families in both Hebron and Jerusalem (see 2 Sam. 3:2–5, 5:14–16).

4. The number twenty includes David and Bathsheba's son who died as a result of God's judgment of their adultery (2 Sam. 12:9–19).

5. Besides children borne by his wives, David also fathered children by his many concubines, although none are specifically named in the Scripture (2 Sam. 5:13, 1 Chron. 3:9).

6. These tragic conflicts within David's family grew out of the sordid soil of his past: his affair with Bathsheba and the murder of her husband Uriah (2 Sam. 11).

pressure cooker of Absalom's heart until at last it spewed forth in an act of vengeance.

> And Absalom commanded his servants, saying, "See now, when Amnon's heart is merry with wine, and when I say to you, 'Strike Amnon,' then put him to death. Do not fear; have not I myself commanded you? Be courageous and be valiant." (v. 28)

4. **Absalom becomes a rebellious runaway.** David was so busy with his job that he was remiss in his responsibilities at home. But finally the problems at home became so out of hand that they intruded upon his professional life. After Absalom murdered his brother, he knew that his father would at last have to step in and deal with the situation. So he fled (vv. 34–39). But the story doesn't stop there. Absalom rallied support to lead a conspiracy against his father in an attempt to wrest the reins of power from David's hands (chaps. 15–17). But the coup failed, and Absalom was killed by Joab (chap. 18, especially vv. 9–15). Upon hearing of Absalom's death, David was pierced to the heart with grief— grief not only over Absalom's death, but about his failure as a father.

> And the king was deeply moved and went up to the chamber over the gate and wept. And thus he said as he walked, "O my son Absalom, my son, my son Absalom! Would I had died instead of you, O Absalom, my son, my son!" (v. 33)

III. Principles for Today

Through his negligence as a father, David had sown the wind, only to later reap the whirlwind. But as the dust settles around the controversies that circled his throne, a few principles for today become clear—principles that can guide our homes.

A. Fight passivity. The pressures of professional and personal life are so demanding that it's easy to neglect the really important things in life—like raising our families. If families are going to hold together, parents have to roll up their sleeves and get involved. No one can be an effective parent *in absentia*. And no one can parent by proxy, delegating the responsibility to someone else.

B. Communicate clearly. Make sure you clearly communicate to your children where the fence lines are—those boundaries for your children's protection—and delineate the consequences of crawling through those fences. And when you're setting those fence posts for your children, be sure to sink them in the concrete of fairness and justice, so they stand straight and true.

C. Discipline firmly. Once a child has crept past a fence that you've established for your home, consistent consequences must follow. Rules lose their effectiveness if they are not enforced. And, in turn, children lose a sense of security when they realize the fences don't mean anything.

D. Maintain authority. Like Absalom, your children will often try to usurp your authority—and in some cases, overthrow it. But when you give in, it may very well result in anarchy. As long as you treat children fairly, they won't threaten your right to rule.

 Living Insights

Study One

The issue is not finding a way to get rid of sibling rivalry but rather learning how to cope with it. Let's study some of the sibling relationships in Scripture to learn some useful coping mechanisms.

- Review the examples of sibling rivalry examined in our lesson. Choose the family most like yours and study it in detail. How could disaster have been avoided? Write down your ideas in the space provided.

Coping with Sibling Rivalry

_____

_____

_____

_____

_____

_____

_____

_____

_____

_____

_____

_____

Living Insights

After a study like this, our thoughts are naturally drawn to our own brothers and sisters. If we're honest, most of us have to admit that we had our share of sibling rivalry. Looking back, some of those memories are pleasant; others, painful. If you could go back in time and relive those relationships, what would you change?

_____

_____

_____

_____

_____

_____

_____

_____

_____

What would you change in your children's relationships with each other so that they will be able to look back years from now with pleasant, rather than painful, memories of their siblings?

_____

_____

_____

_____

_____

_____

_____

_____

_____

Section Three:

WISDOM NEEDED FOR BUILDING THE STRUCTURE

Shaping the Will with Wisdom
Selected Proverbs

In his excellent book *The Strong-Willed Child,* Dr. James Dobson describes the inevitable tug-of-war between the parent's will and the child's.

> It is obvious that children are aware of the contest of wills between generations, and that is precisely why the parental response is so important. When a child behaves in ways that are disrespectful or harmful to himself or others, his hidden purpose is often to verify the stability of the boundaries. This testing has much the same function as a policeman who turns doorknobs at places of business after dark. Though he tries to open doors, he hopes they are locked and secure. Likewise, a child who assaults the loving authority of his parents is greatly reassured when their leadership holds firm and confident. He finds his greatest security in a structured environment where the rights of other people (and his own) are protected by definite boundaries.[1]

The objective in child rearing is not for parents to win the tug-of-war at all costs. For if you do, you may end up not only with a muddy, tearful child but also with a relationship strained beyond repair. Rather, your objective is to shape the will, gently yet firmly, as a potter would a clay vase. But that takes a special kind of wisdom—a wisdom only God can provide.

I. Some Necessary Distinctions Worth Making
Proverbs, a veritable storehouse of godly wisdom, tells us that if we truly love our children, we'll discipline them diligently (13:24). But since the word *discipline* is so emotionally charged and so generally misunderstood, we need to make some distinctions that will help clarify the concept.

   A. Between abuse and discipline. Because child abuse has reached tragic proportions today, many people avoid any kind

1. James Dobson, *The Strong-Willed Child* (Wheaton, Ill.: Tyndale House Publishers, 1978), p. 30. Used by permission.

of discipline. But there is a difference: abuse tears down a child's spirit; discipline builds it up.

1. **Abuse is unfair, extreme, and degrading.** It's unduly harsh, unnecessarily long, and totally inappropriate. When you drag a child's feelings through the mud and kick him when he's down, you're being abusive. The result? A soiled self-esteem and scars that often last a lifetime. Actions like that are not discipline; they're abuse. And abuse doesn't grow out of love; it stems from hate.

2. **Discipline is fair, fitting, and upholds the child's dignity.** Discipline is built on a foundation of justice. It isn't capricious or arbitrary, so the child has a good idea of the punishment that will be meted out after willfully and defiantly violating parental boundaries. This form of correction strengthens rather than shatters the child's self-worth. Discipline is rooted in proper motivation—love and genuine concern—not in anger or expedience.

B. **Between crushing and shaping.** Proverbs 15:13 paints a vivid contrast between a spirit that has been shaped and one that has been crushed.

A joyful heart makes a cheerful face,
But when the heart is sad, the spirit is broken.

Proverbs 17:22 cameos a relief of a similar image.

A joyful heart is good medicine,
But a broken spirit dries up the bones.

The ultimate goal of discipline is to build up your children with direction and confidence, giving them a strong and secure self-esteem to carry them through life. Shaping the will nurtures a vitality for living, while crushing the will "dries up" that vitality.

C. **Between natural childishness and willful defiance.** Every child needs space in which to learn, make mistakes, and develop in the early years of growing up. As a parent, it's important for you to distinguish between childish irresponsibility and behavior that is willfully disobedient. Again, Dr. Dobson has some insightful wisdom on the subject.

A child should not be spanked for behavior that is not willfully defiant. When he forgets to feed the dog or make his bed or take out the trash—when he leaves your tennis racket outside in the rain or loses his bicycle—remember that these behaviors are typical of childhood. It is, more than likely, the mechanism by which an immature mind is protected from adult anxieties and pressures. Be gentle as you teach him to do better. If he fails to respond to your patient instruction, it then becomes appropriate to administer some well-defined consequences (he may have to work to pay for the item he abused or be deprived of its use, etc.). However, childish irresponsibility is very different from willful defiance, and should be handled more patiently.[2]

II. Several Suggestions Worth Considering

Shaping the will with wisdom is a critical task of parenting. Here are some suggestions that should make it easier and more effective.

A. Start early. We look again to Proverbs for wisdom to carry out this awesome responsibility. In 13:24 Solomon provides some practical hints.

He who spares his rod hates his son,
But he who loves him disciplines him diligently.

The word *diligently* has a colorful background in the Hebrew. Originally, it meant "dawn" or "early morning." Later it evolved into the idea of pursuing something early in life—like a career—and thus came to mean "with determination" or "with diligence." The association of *diligence* with *discipline* indicates that we should start disciplining our children early in their lives. The longer we wait to begin the process, the more difficult it will become (compare 19:18).

B. Stay balanced. Balance is what keeps children from falling off their bicycles and skinning their knees. Balance also keeps parents from crashing when it comes to discipline. Two kinds of discipline are mentioned in the Bible. Both complement each other, but both must be kept in balance.

   1. Physical discipline. Proverbs 22:15 describes this category of discipline.

Foolishness is bound up in the heart of a child;
The rod of discipline[3] will remove it far from him.

The rod indicates the infliction of pain. Once again we turn to Dr. Dobson as he underscores the importance of the child being able to associate wrongdoing with pain.

If your child has ever bumped his arm against a hot stove, you can bet he'll never deliberately do that again. He does not become a more violent person because the stove burnt him; in fact, he learned a valuable lesson from the pain. Similarly, when he falls out of his high chair or smashes his finger in the door or is bitten by a

---

2. Dobson, *The Strong-Willed Child,* p. 32. Used by permission.
3. The Hebrew root is *yasar.*

grumpy dog, he learns about physical dangers in his world. These bumps and bruises throughout childhood are nature's way of teaching him what to fear. They do not damage his self-esteem. They do not make him vicious. They merely acquaint him with reality. In like manner, an appropriate spanking from a loving parent provides the same service. It tells him there are not only physical dangers to be avoided, but he must steer clear of some social traps as well (selfishness, defiance, dishonesty, unprovoked aggression, etc.).[4]

2. **Verbal discipline.** The category of correction known as reproof is found in Proverbs 3:11–12.

My son, do not reject the discipline of the Lord,
Or loathe His reproof,[5]
For whom the Lord loves He reproves,
Even as a father, the son in whom he delights.

Reproof is not a tongue-lashing with cutting remarks that lacerate character. It is verbal instruction arising out of a genuine and deep-felt delight in the child (note the word *delights* in verse 12). Proverbs 29:15 shows verbal reproof in balance with physical discipline: "The rod and reproof give wisdom."

C. **Be consistent.** When you're under pressure, it's easy to let expediency determine how and when you discipline your child—a case of the urgent squeezing out the important. But the rule shouldn't be expediency; it should be consistency. Here are a few guidelines to ensure that your discipline will be consistent.

—Make sure the rules are known beforehand.
—Discipline privately.
—Explain the violation and its consequences.
—Administer the rod soundly.
—Tenderly hold your child after the spanking.
—Assure your child of your love and concern.

D. **Be reasonable.** As a child grows older, there comes a time when it is inappropriate to use the rod. If you're not sensitive to this, you will end up demeaning rather than disciplining your child.

---

4. James Dobson, *Hide or Seek,* rev. ed. (Old Tappan, N.J.: Fleming H. Revell Co., 1979), p 95. Used by permission.

5. The Hebrew root is *yakach.*

III. Significant Goals Worth Implementing

You may miss the mark on discipline from time to time, but if you don't have a goal in sight, you're likely to miss every time you try. To stay on target, here are a couple of goals to aim at.

A. For yourself. Model God's role of authority until your child reaches the point where there is a natural transfer of that authority from you to God.

B. For your children. Help them cultivate a healthy respect for themselves and others so they can be strong enough and secure enough to perform well under the pressures of life.

 Living Insights

Study One ▬▬▬▬▬▬▬▬▬▬▬▬▬▬▬▬▬▬▬▬▬▬

The book of Proverbs is loaded with nuggets of truth concerning the discipline of children. Let's go exploring for some of this gold!

- With the help of a concordance, conduct a Scripture search through Proverbs on the subject of discipline. Look up words like *discipline, correct,* and *rod.* Write your findings in the space that follows.

Discipline: A Scripture Search	
Verses	Discoveries

64

Living Insights

A fascinating relationship usually exists between how you were disciplined as a child and how you discipline your own children. Using the suggestions made in this study, reflect on how your parents disciplined you.

- Start early.

- Stay balanced.

- Be consistent.

- Be reasonable.

If you have children at home, write out how you can use these suggestions to wisely discipline them.

_____

_____

_____

_____

_____

_____

_____

_____

_____

_____

_____

_____

_____

Ways to Enhance Esteem

Ephesians 5:25–30, Selected Proverbs

One of the greatest contributions family members can make to one another is to enhance each person's self-esteem. Odds are, if it doesn't happen at home, it probably won't happen at all.

Unfortunately, families are often better at putting each other down than building each other up. They use their words as swords rather than scalpels, to hurt rather than heal.

There is one who speaks rashly like the thrusts of a sword,
But the tongue of the wise brings healing. (Prov. 12:18)

Contrary to the childhood chant, "Sticks and stones may break my bones, but words will never hurt me," cutting words do hurt. They penetrate deeply into a person's heart, slashing self-esteem to ribbons.

In today's lesson, rather than explore ways to eviscerate esteem, we'll examine some ways to enhance it.

I. Essential Value of Self-Esteem

Ephesians 5:25–30 is a foundational passage of Scripture in determining the value of self-esteem. Though this passage focuses on the marriage relationship, its principle is universal.

Husbands, love your wives, just as Christ also loved the church and gave Himself up for her; that He might sanctify her, having cleansed her by the washing of water with the word, that He might present to Himself the church in all her glory, having no spot or wrinkle or any such thing; but that she should be holy and blameless. So husbands ought also to love their own wives as their own bodies. (vv. 25–28a)

The universal principle is this: the love we show our wives, or anyone else, is in direct proportion to the love we have for ourselves. And this love for ourselves is not a noisy conceit, but a quiet sense of self-worth.

A. Components of its development. Verses 28b–30 give parents two important actions to enhance the development of self-esteem in their children.

He who loves his own wife loves himself; for no one ever hated his own flesh, but nourishes and cherishes it, just as Christ also does the church, because we are members of His body.

1. Nourish. The Greek word is *ektrephō*. Its root, *trephō,* means "to bring," and the prefix *ek* means "out." It is most often used in a context relating to children, as in Ephesians 6:4, and has the idea of feeding, caring for, and drawing out the child. The word implies that there are things deep within the child which parents should draw out.

2. **Cherish.** The Greek word here is *thalpō,* meaning "to heat or keep warm." It's a picture of tenderness, holding someone close to keep them warm. In the Greek translation of the Hebrew Old Testament, called the Septuagint, it is used of a bird sitting on her eggs (Deut. 22:6). In the New Testament it is used of the tenderness of a nursing mother (1 Thess. 2:7). Putting the two components of nourishing and cherishing together conveys the distinct impression that enhancing your child's self-esteem requires a great amount of attention and affection. Within every child are certain God-given characteristics. As those characteristics are "drawn out" and "warmed," the self-esteem of that child begins to grow stronger.

B. **Compensations for its absence.** When self-esteem is lacking, people often put up defenses—covering up, rationalizing, or aggressively asserting themselves. They may also wear masks—a plastic smile or a constant frown—to hide their hurt or insecurity. It's been said: "Scratch a humorist and you'll find a sad man." Humor often becomes a mask for a hurting person to hide behind. Ask any comedian. Onstage humor stems from offstage hurt, a truth Proverbs 14:13 corroborates—"Even in laughter the heart may be in pain."

C. **Culmination of its presence.** When your children have strong self-esteem, they are free to be everything God created them to be. They can accept and love others because they have first accepted and loved themselves. And they will have a calm sense of security and a deep sense of satisfaction independent of performance or peer recognition.

Watch Your Words

Are you committed to giving your children the invaluable gift of a strong self-worth? If so, it will be reflected in your words. Words like, "Nice job, Son" or "Thanks, Honey. That was so thoughtful of you."

Are those the words that greet your children when they come home from school? Or do the words "How many times have I told you . . ." or "Do it right or don't do it at all" cut into their tender hearts?

Remember, life and death are in the power of the tongue—the life of your child's self-esteem, or its death.

II. Biblical Insights on Cultivating Self-Esteem

Returning to Ephesians 5, we see both a theological basis and a philosophical framework for cultivating self-esteem.

A. Theological basis. Verses 28–29 suggest two crucial points. First, a good self-esteem is God's desire for us because it provides the foundation to love others. And second, God sees worth and value in each of us, for we are nourished and cherished by Christ.

B. Philosophical framework. Verses 25–30 answer the question, "Why should we love ourselves?"

> Husbands, love your wives, just as Christ also loved the church and gave Himself up for her. (v. 25)

Loving ourselves enables us to unselfishly love others. It also allows us to bring out the best in others, as Christ does with us,

> that He might present to Himself the church in all her glory, having no spot or wrinkle or any such thing; but that she should be holy and blameless. (v. 27)

Finally, it helps us to be more like Christ Himself.

> For no one ever hated his own flesh, but nourishes and cherishes it, just as Christ also does the church, because we are members of His body. (vv. 29–30)

C. Practical suggestions. From the wealth of Proverbs come three gems of wisdom, parental qualities your children will treasure forever.

1. **A commitment to discover.** Deep within the heart are concealed the secrets of one's life, caved away like a subterranean spring. Parents, therefore, must be committed to digging down deep and drawing out that sparkling water hidden in their children.

   > A plan in the heart of a man is like deep water,
   > But a man of understanding draws it out. (Prov. 20:5)

2. **A willingness to get involved.** As a file hones the edges of a knife, so a sharpening of the soul occurs when two people intimately and intensely interact.

   > Iron sharpens iron,
   > So one man sharpens another. (27:17)

   If your family wants to sharpen each other emotionally, you have to get involved emotionally. If you want to sharpen each other spiritually, you must get involved spiritually. If you want to sharpen each other mentally, you have to get involved mentally. You need to be there for your children, actively helping them grow.

3. **An ability to reflect.** Just as we need mirrors around the house to see if our hair is in place, so we need family members to reflect our inner self in order for us to see what's going on inside. In that reflection is where our identity comes into focus.

> As in water face reflects face,
> So the heart of man reflects man. (27:19)

We also see just how much we are valued in their eyes. And as water reflects best when calm and still, so do we.

III. Personal Ways to Encourage Self-Esteem

By now, you may be asking *how.* How do I, as a parent, discover my child? How do I get involved? How do I reflect? Here are two ways to help do those things and thus encourage your child's self-worth.

A. **Develop good, open communication.** Not churchy little homilies complete with organ accompaniment; but real talk for the real world. Not pious words from the pulpit; but transparent teaching from your own life.

B. **Help each child compensate.** Find an area of strength in your children's lives, and help them develop it to compensate for weaker areas. If your child isn't athletic, for example, focus on artistic or musical development. Help your children discover their unique, God-given abilities and talents.

A Concluding Thought

Roy Croft, in his poem "Love," shows how love cherishes and nourishes . . . how it discovers, gets involved, and reflects . . . how it draws out and develops the loved one's self-esteem.

> I love you,
> Not only for what you are,
> But for what I am
> When I am with you.
>
> I love you,
> Not only for what
> You have made of yourself,
> But for what
> You are making of me.
>
> I love you,
> For the part of me
> That you bring out;
> I love you
> For putting your hand
> Into my heaped-up heart

And passing over
All the foolish, weak things
That you can't help
Dimly seeing there,
And for drawing out
Into the light
All the beautiful belongings
That no one else had looked
Quite far enough to find.

I love you because you
Are helping me to make
Of the lumber of my life
Not a tavern
But a temple;
Out of the works
Of my every day
Not a reproach
But a song.[1]

 Living Insights

Study One ▬▬▬▬▬▬▬▬▬▬▬▬▬▬▬▬▬▬▬▬▬▬

Ephesians 5 lines up next in family importance to Deuteronomy 6, a chapter we studied earlier. Since we gleaned so much from paraphrasing Deuteronomy 6, let's do the same with the Ephesians passage we studied today.

_____

_____

_____

_____

_____

_____

_____

_____

1. Roy Croft, as quoted in *The Best Loved Poems of the American People*, selected by Hazel Felleman (Garden City, N.Y.: Doubleday and Co., 1936), p. 25.

_____

_____

_____

_____

_____

_____

_____

_____

_____

_____

_____

_____

🌳 Living Insights

Study Two ━━━━━━━━━━━━━━━━━━━━━━━━━━

At some time God has probably placed in your life at least one person who believed in you, encouraged you, and helped you realize your worth. Have you ever communicated your appreciation to that special person?

● Send a note of thanks to the person who gave you hope. It may be a brief card or a lengthy letter, but make sure you communicate how this person helped develop your feelings of self-worth and how that's made a difference in your life.

Change: Challenging Years of Adolescence
Selected Scripture

Adolescence. Could there be a more difficult time in life? Hormones race through your body like horses out of a starting gate. A huge pimple erupts on your nose the day of The Big Date. Your voice cracks to broadcast that you're still not a man yet.

This time of transition closes the door on your childhood. Baseball cards give way to drivers' licenses. Dolls give way to boyfriends. Dress-up gives way to the prom. Lazy vacation days give way to summer jobs.

Childhood is behind you, forever locked away. And there you stand on the threshold of adult life, biting your nails. Your knees are knocking, and it seems the entire world is watching as you take that uncertain first step. All the while, your body is giving you a shove. And with a thud you stumble unceremoniously into adulthood.

I. Some Significant Questions Adolescents Ask

During this slippery time, it is no wonder adolescents begin exchanging exclamation points for question marks. In groping to find their balance and stand on their own two feet, they question even the very ground that supports them. The questions are legion, but they generally fall into four main categories.

A. Who am I? This first question emerges out of the struggle adolescents have with *identity*. As everything begins to change in a teenager's life, the question "Who is the real me?" becomes central.

B. What attitudes will I choose? Prior to adolescence a child learns to be submissive to Mom and Dad. But as the child begins to grow up, the question of *responsibility* is raised. In childhood, the consequences of irresponsible behavior were buffered. Adulthood, however, has a way of exacting consequences from the irresponsible decisions we make. Adolescents want the right to be independent, but they struggle with accepting the attendant responsibilities.

C. Whose role will I respect? This question involves the struggle over *authority*. As adolescents try to discover where they fit into society, they also begin to question the pillars of authority undergirding that society. Authority figures are everywhere: parents, teachers, principals, coaches, policemen, employers. "Whom do I follow? How far? And for how long?" Questions like these peck away at a teenager's thinking.

D. What will be my lifestyle? Up until now children have adopted their parents' values. If their parents avoid alcohol, they do too. If their parents go to church, they go along. If their parents value education, so do they. But when adolescence emerges, everything is up for grabs. The struggle becomes one of *conformity*. They ask themselves, "Which road will my life take? The way of my parents? My peers? The public? Will I be a follower and adopt their lifestyle, or will I chart a path of my own?"

II. The Struggles of Two Adolescents in the Bible

To demonstrate that the struggles of adolescence aren't confined to those in our generation, let's go back in time to examine two other adolescents, Jephthah and Absalom. As we take a look at some incidents in their adolescent days, we'll see how their response to those incidents helped shape their adult life.

A. Jephthah. Judges 11 introduces him to us.

> Now Jephthah the Gileadite was a valiant warrior, but he was the son of a harlot. And Gilead was the father of Jephthah. And Gilead's wife bore him sons; and when his wife's sons grew up, they drove Jephthah out and said to him, "You shall not have an inheritance in our father's house, for you are the son of another woman." So Jephthah fled from his brothers and lived in the land of Tob; and worthless fellows gathered themselves about Jephthah, and they went out with him. (vv. 1–3)

Unwanted and rejected, Jephthah struggled with identity. Cut out of the will and kicked out of the home, he no doubt asked himself, "Who am I?" For an answer he turned to his friends, a gang of good-for-nothings that Proverbs warns against in 1:10–19. And while he's hanging out with these hoods, he's on a quiet but desperate search for himself. Even as an adult, Jephthah still searched for identity and needed acceptance. That's what made the offer appealing to be leader over all who lived in Gilead (Judg. 11:9), despite his deep feelings of resentment.

> And it came about after a while that the sons of Ammon fought against Israel. And it happened when the sons of Ammon fought against Israel that the elders of Gilead went to get Jephthah from the land of Tob; and they said to Jephthah, "Come and be our chief that we may fight against the sons of Ammon." Then Jephthah said to the elders of Gilead, "Did you not hate me and drive me from my father's house?

So why have you come to me now when you are in trouble?" And the elders of Gilead said to Jephthah, "For this reason we have now returned to you, that you may go with us and fight with the sons of Ammon and become head over all the inhabitants of Gilead." So Jephthah said to the elders of Gilead, "If you take me back to fight against the sons of Ammon and the Lord gives them up to me, will I become your head?" And the elders of Gilead said to Jephthah, "The Lord is witness between us; surely we will do as you have said." Then Jephthah went with the elders of Gilead, and the people made him head and chief over them; and Jephthah spoke all his words before the Lord at Mizpah. (vv. 4–11)

The Influence of Friends

Solomon instructed his son:
He who walks with wise men will be wise,
But the companion of fools will suffer harm.
(Prov. 13:20)
Jephthah fell into the companionship of fools—"worthless fellows," says Scripture. Do you know who your children's companions are? Have you ever talked with them about the qualities of a good friend? Are you equipping them to make good decisions regarding their choice of friends? You should be, if you want to help them grow wisely into adulthood. For the shape of your children's future is molded largely by those who surround them, which will most likely be their peers rather than their parents.

B. Absalom. After the rape of his sister by their half brother Amnon and the passive response of his father, Absalom was left with a jigsaw of puzzling attitudes to fit together. One thing he puzzled over was responsibility—"What attitude should I choose?" For two years resentment stirred in Absalom's heart toward his father David. And for two years hatred toward Amnon simmered, until it turned into a rolling boil. At last, that seething cauldron of resentment and hatred spilled over into an act of vengeance.

And Absalom commanded his servants, saying, "See now, when Amnon's heart is merry with wine, and when I say to you, 'Strike Amnon,' then put him to death. Do not fear; have not I myself commanded you? Be courageous and be valiant." (2 Sam. 13:28)

As it was commanded, so it was done (v. 29). And after the murder, Absalom fled.

> Now Absalom fled and went to Talmai the son of Ammihud, the king of Geshur. And David mourned for his son every day. (v. 37)

To whom did he run? To Talmai, his maternal grandfather (2 Sam. 3:3). And for what was he looking? Roots, security, direction. For three years Absalom stayed with Talmai (13:38). Then, after some persuasion from Joab, David had Absalom brought back to Jerusalem . . . but something was wrong.

> The king said, "Let him turn to his own house, and let him not see my face." So Absalom turned to his own house and did not see the king's face. (14:24)

After a three-year absence, you would think Absalom and David would have wanted to see each other, talk things out, make things right. But a wall of resentment stood between them. For two years Absalom lived in Jerusalem, and for two years that wall remained (v. 28). As Absalom grew from adolescence to adulthood, he attempted to hurdle that wall in an effort to see his father and remove the bitter stones that stood between them.

> Then Absalom sent for Joab, to send him to the king, but he would not come to him. So he sent again a second time, but he would not come. Therefore he said to his servants, "See, Joab's field is next to mine, and he has barley there; go and set it on fire." So Absalom's servants set the field on fire. Then Joab arose, came to Absalom at his house and said to him, "Why have your servants set my field on fire?" And Absalom answered Joab, "Behold, I sent for you, saying, 'Come here, that I may send you to the king, to say, "Why have I come from Geshur? It would be better for me still to be there."' Now therefore, let me see the king's face; and if there is iniquity in me, let him put me to death." (vv. 29–32)

So Joab agreed to take Absalom's request to the king.

> When Joab came to the king and told him, he called for Absalom. Thus he came to the king and prostrated himself on his face to the ground before the king, and the king kissed Absalom. (v. 33)

But seeing his father didn't tear down the wall between them. Nothing was revealed of their talking things out or making things right—only a kiss. And even that was nondescript and apparently without feeling. This perfunctory kiss pushed Absalom over the edge and set him on a collision course with his father.

Now it came about after this that Absalom provided for himself a chariot and horses, and fifty men as runners before him. And Absalom used to rise early and stand beside the way to the gate; and it happened that when any man had a suit to come to the king for judgment, Absalom would call to him and say, "From what city are you?" And he would say, "Your servant is from one of the tribes of Israel." Then Absalom would say to him, "See, your claims are good and right, but no man listens to you on the part of the king." Moreover, Absalom would say, "Oh that one would appoint me judge in the land, then every man who has any suit or cause could come to me, and I would give him justice." And it happened that when a man came near to prostrate himself before him, he would put out his hand and take hold of him and kiss him. And in this manner Absalom dealt with all Israel who came to the king for judgment; so Absalom stole away the hearts of the men of Israel. (15:1–6)

With those stolen hearts, Absalom forged an insurrection. But Absalom sent spies throughout all the tribes of Israel, saying, "As soon as you hear the sound of the trumpet, then you shall say, 'Absalom is king in Hebron.' " Then two hundred men went with Absalom from Jerusalem, who were invited and went innocently, and they did not know anything. And Absalom sent for Ahithophel the Gilonite, David's counselor, from his city Giloh, while he was offering the sacrifices. And the conspiracy was strong, for the people increased continually with Absalom. (vv. 10–12)

And if anarchy weren't enough of a dagger to thrust in his father's heart, Absalom twisted the blade with a personal affront. Then Absalom said to Ahithophel, "Give your advice. What shall we do?" And Ahithophel said to Absalom, "Go in to your father's concubines, whom he has left to keep the house; then all Israel will hear that you have made yourself odious to your father. The hands of all who are with you will also be strengthened." So they pitched a tent for Absalom on the roof, and Absalom went in to his father's concubines in the sight of all Israel. (16:20–22)

Earlier, Absalom chose the attitudes of resentment, rebellion, and retaliation. Later, he refused to repent. Finally, he openly revolted against his father's authority.

III. Insights for Parents to Ponder

A. Few things are more damaging to an adolescent than rejection. Jephthah is a case in point. It's hard enough to struggle with identity and self-esteem at this age, but feeling rejected makes those difficult times virtually impossible. As a parent, try to be especially affirming during your child's adolescent years. And try not to condemn. Remember, "the tongue of the wise brings healing" (Prov. 12:18b).

B. Few things are more essential to an adolescent than communication. This was what Absalom wanted so desperately from his father—but he never got it. The king was busy. The king was tired. The king was talked out after a long day at the throne. Consequently, one opportunity after another slipped through David's fingers. Until it was too late . . . and he saw his son slip away forever.

 Living Insights

Study One ━━━━━━━━━━━━━━━━━━━━━━━━━━━━━━━

As Psalm 1 says, there are two roads that we can travel in life: the way of the righteous and the way of the wicked. The one leads to life under the watchful eye of God. The other leads to death under the wrathful glare of God.

It's obvious from our study which road Jephthah and Absalom took. If you had the chance to rewrite history, what would you change about the decisions they made during their adolescent years? When you answer, think in terms of the categories at the beginning of our lesson: identity and responsibility.

● How could Jephthah have resolved the "Who am I?" question better than he did? What decisions could he have made that would have put his early life on a better road?

_____

_____

_____

_____

_____

_____

Continued on next page

_____

_____

_____

_____

_____

_____

Fortunately, Jephthah did take a right turn later in his life and ended up on a better road. He not only became a well-respected judge but became known as a man of faith (Heb. 11:32).

- How could Absalom have resolved the "What attitude will I choose?" question better than he did? What decisions could he have made that would have put his life on a better road?

_____

_____

_____

_____

_____

_____

_____

_____

_____

_____

_____

In contrast to Jephthah, Absalom stayed on the road to destruction and was murdered by his father's ally Joab (2 Sam. 18:9–15).

Living Insights

It's pretty easy to lash out at today's teenagers. But before we go to town on them, let's ask this question . . . what were the teenage years like for you?

● Take a few minutes to write about your memories of life as an adolescent. Write about both the good and the bad. Be as honest and insightful as you can.

My Life as an Adolescent

_____

_____

_____

_____

_____

_____

_____

_____

_____

_____

_____

_____

_____

_____

_____

_____

_____

_____

_____

_____

Another Look at Adolescence
2 Chronicles 34:1–21, Daniel 1:3–20

Jim Conway's book *Men in Mid-Life Crisis* refers to the period of mid-life as a "second adolescence." In developing that idea, Conway points out four major enemies of a man in the throes of that crisis.

Enemy number one: his body. He is losing his hair, losing his looks, and losing his physique. Odds are, the only thing he isn't losing is weight.

Enemy number two: his work. The thrill of his job is quietly replaced by monotony. He often asks himself: "How in the world did I ever get stuck in a job like this?"

Enemy number three: his wife and family. His responsibilities at home make him feel trapped. Even though he wants to find a more fulfilling career, he can't leave his job and forget about his family's needs.

Enemy number four: his God. The man in mid-life pictures God leaning over the pulpit of heaven, pointing an accusatory finger, and preaching incriminations at him: "You're selfish, you're lazy, and you're filled with lust." In response, the man lashes back and blames God for giving him his frail body, along with its drives and weaknesses.

Yes, second adolescence is not a bad label for those going through a mid-life crisis. And it tells us a lot about how adolescents feel as well. Similar to mid-life men, they, too, have four major enemies: identity, responsibility, authority, and conformity. We covered the first two in the previous lesson. Now we'll examine the last two.

I. Two Questions—Two Teens

Teenagers wrestle with a number of questions as they go through the traumatic transition of adolescence. Two of those questions concern authority and conformity. And two teenagers whose lives lived out right answers to those questions were Josiah and Daniel.

A. Josiah. Josiah's grandfather, King Manasseh, ruled Judah for fifty-five years. During most of that time he led the people away from God. Following on the heels of Manasseh came Josiah's father Amon. The final verses of 2 Chronicles 33 document both his morally destitute character and his mutinied demise.

Amon was twenty-two years old when he became king, and he reigned two years in Jerusalem. And he did evil in the sight of the Lord as Manasseh his father had done, and Amon sacrificed to all the carved images which his father Manasseh had made, and he served them. Moreover, he did not humble himself before the Lord as his father Manasseh had done, but Amon multiplied guilt. Finally his servants conspired against him and put him to death in his own house. (vv. 21–24)

To fill the throne, the people looked to eight-year-old Josiah. Remarkably, considering his family tree, Josiah developed an unswerving obedience to God (34:2). Instead of throwing off the yoke of the Lord, like his father and grandfather had done, Josiah chose to follow the role model of another predecessor.

For in the eighth year of his reign while he was still a youth, he began to seek the God of his father David. (v. 3a)

The Hebrew word for *seek* is *darash.* It means "to seek with care, to inquire, to search out." Josiah made a serious, diligent search to know God. As a result, he made a conscious decision that the Lord would be his authority and he would listen to His counsel. And first and foremost on God's list was to purify the country by eliminating idolatry.

And in the twelfth year he began to purge Judah and Jerusalem of the high places, the Asherim, the carved images, and the molten images. And they tore down the altars of the Baals in his presence, and the incense altars that were high above them he chopped down; also the Asherim, the carved images, and the molten images he broke in pieces and ground to powder and scattered it on the graves of those who had sacrificed to them. (vv. 3b–4)

Fresh out of adolescence, Josiah stood up and put an end to two generations of wickedness. What is it that molds a man like that? Whatever it was, we know it didn't come from his father. Second Kings 22:1 provides a clue.

Josiah was eight years old when he became king, and he reigned thirty-one years in Jerusalem; and his mother's name was Jedidah the daughter of Adaiah of Bozkath.

Usually the new ruler's father is listed in these biblical accounts of the kings. But here we see Josiah's mother. Why? Probably because she was the primary influence in his life. In 2 Chronicles 34 we pick up Josiah at twenty-six and see an incredible heart for the things of God—a heart his mother probably helped cultivate.

Now in the eighteenth year of his reign, when he had purged the land and the house, he sent Shaphan the son of Azaliah, and Maaseiah an official of the city, and Joah the son of Joahaz the recorder, to repair the house of the Lord his God. And they came to Hilkiah the high priest and delivered the money that was brought into the house of God, which the Levites, the doorkeepers, had collected from Manasseh and Ephraim, and from all the remnant of Israel, and from all Judah and Benjamin and the inhabitants of Jerusalem. . . . When they were bringing out the money which had been brought into the house of the Lord, Hilkiah the priest found the book of the law of the Lord given by Moses. And Hilkiah responded and said to Shaphan the scribe, "I have found the book of the law in the house of the Lord." And Hilkiah gave the book to Shaphan. . . . Shaphan the scribe told the king saying, "Hilkiah the priest gave me a book." And Shaphan read from it in the presence of the king. And it came about when the king heard the words of the law that he tore his clothes. Then the king commanded Hilkiah, Ahikam the son of Shaphan, Abdon the son of Micah, Shaphan the scribe, and Asaiah the king's servant, saying, "Go, inquire of the Lord for me and for those who are left in Israel and in Judah, concerning the words of the book which has been found; for great is the wrath of the Lord which is poured out on us because our fathers have not observed the word of the Lord, to do according to all that is written in this book." (vv. 8–9, 14–15, 18–21)

A Thought to Consider

Parents—don't underestimate the influence of your son or daughter. If Josiah could change a nation, your child can change the course of a peer group, or even an entire school.

B. Daniel. As a young man, Daniel struggled successfully with the question of conformity. Most of us remember Daniel from the lions' den. But we forget that the steel-tempered courage of Daniel's later life was forged on the anvil of his adolescence. For it was during Daniel's adolescence that he and his Jewish countrymen were taken captive to Babylon by Nebuchadnezzar.

Then the king ordered Ashpenaz, the chief of his officials, to bring in some of the sons of Israel, including some of the royal family and of the nobles, youths in whom was no defect, who were good-looking, showing intelligence in every branch of wisdom,

endowed with understanding, and discerning knowledge, and who had ability for serving in the king's
court; and he ordered him to teach them the literature and language of the Chaldeans. (Dan. 1:3–4)
What is Nebuchadnezzar trying to do? To mold them into good
Babylonian citizens. These monotheistic, straight-laced Jewish
boys are brought to the big city with its enormous pressure to
conform. And then they're given a crash course in Babylonian
life.

And the king appointed for them a daily ration from
the king's choice food and from the wine which he
drank, and appointed that they should be educated
three years, at the end of which they were to enter
the king's personal service. (v. 5)
So great was the pressure to conform that they were even given
new names—Babylonian names (vv. 6–7). But Daniel was determined not to let his external label affect his inner commitment to God.

Daniel made up his mind that he would not defile
himself with the king's choice food or with the wine
which he drank. (v. 8a)
So Daniel proposed a test.

He sought permission from the commander of the
officials that he might not defile himself. Now God
granted Daniel favor and compassion in the sight of
the commander of the officials, and the commander
of the officials said to Daniel, "I am afraid of my
lord the king, who has appointed your food and your
drink; for why should he see your faces looking more
haggard than the youths who are your own age? Then
you would make me forfeit my head to the king." But
Daniel said to the overseer whom the commander of
the officials had appointed over Daniel, Hananiah,
Mishael and Azariah, "Please test your servants for
ten days, and let us be given some vegetables to eat
and water to drink. Then let our appearance be observed in your presence, and the appearance of the
youths who are eating the king's choice food; and
deal with your servants according to what you see."
(vv. 8b–13)
With some skepticism, no doubt, the overseer agreed to a ten-
day trial run.

And at the end of ten days their appearance seemed
better and they were fatter than all the youths who

had been eating the king's choice food. So the overseer continued to withhold their choice food and the
wine they were to drink, and kept giving them vegetables. (vv. 15–16)

Finishing the king's course of study, Daniel graduated valedic-
torian, with his three friends following right behind him.

And as for these four youths, God gave them knowledge and intelligence in every branch of literature
and wisdom; Daniel even understood all kinds of
visions and dreams. Then at the end of the days
which the king had specified for presenting them, the
commander of the officials presented them before
Nebuchadnezzar. And the king talked with them,
and out of them all not one was found like Daniel,
Hananiah, Mishael and Azariah; so they entered the
king's personal service. And as for every matter of
wisdom and understanding about which the king
consulted them, he found them ten times better than
all the magicians and conjurers who were in all his
realm. (vv. 17–20)

The secret to Daniel's unique favor with the Lord? He made
up his mind that he wouldn't defile himself. And he followed
through with that commitment.

II. Two Practical Lessons

These two remarkable teenagers—Josiah and Daniel—wrestled and
triumphed over the questions of authority and conformity. From
them we can learn two practical lessons.

**A. Adolescents must be given room to make up their
minds.** You've got to give them room—even if that means they
fail. Your counsel is valuable. Your support is valuable. Your
influence is valuable. But taking your hand away and letting
them walk on their own two feet is also valuable. And you must
do that if they will ever learn to walk.

**B. Personal convictions stand the test better than forced
convictions.** From dieting to doctrinal statements, adults know
the reality of this lesson. When you decide something based on
your deep inner convictions, you will better handle any temptations and trials than if those convictions were forced on you.
The same is true for teenagers. Share your convictions, but don't
be dictatorial. Patiently allow your teenagers to explore and
develop their own convictions.

84

Living Insights

In his excellent book *The Screwtape Letters,* C. S. Lewis writes about the process God uses to raise his children.

He wants them to learn to walk and must therefore take away His hand; and if only the will to walk is really there He is pleased even with their stumbles.

One lesson we learned in our study is that adolescents must be given room to make up their own minds. In giving them room and taking away your hand, they are more vulnerable to a fall. But remember, it is in falling that we learn to go safely. Be there to pick them up and dust them off, but don't hold their hands through all the tough decision in life. Give them room. Give them a chance to think on their own.

Is there some area of your children's lives in which you are still taking them by the hand? Think through the following areas and see what you can do to help your children think more independently.

MONEY _____

_____

_____

MUSIC _____

_____

_____

CLOTHES _____

_____

_____

CHURCH _____

_____

_____

FRIENDS _____

_____

_____

1. C. S. Lewis, *The Screwtape Letters* (New York, N.Y.: Macmillan Publishing Co., 1961), p. 39.

Living Insights

We've come far enough in our study to merit a breather. Let's pause to review—an excellent way to underscore what we've learned.

• Let's review our learning from Scripture. Next to each lesson title, write the biblical truth that touched you most in that particular lesson, and summarize one way you applied it.

Wisdom Used in Appraising the Scene

Danger Signals of a Disintegrating Family _____

_____

_____

_____

Is Yours a Genuinely Christian Family? _____

_____

_____

_____

Wisdom Applied to Cultivating the Soil

Dads, Front and Center _____

_____

_____

_____

Mothers: An Endangered Species _____

_____

_____

_____

Mom and Dad . . . Meet Your Child _____

_____

_____

_____

The Bents in Your Baby _____

_____

_____

_____

A Chip off the Old Bent _____

_____

_____

_____

When Brothers and Sisters Battle _____

_____

_____

_____

Wisdom Needed for Building the Structure

Shaping the Will with Wisdom _____

_____

_____

_____

Ways to Enhance Esteem _____

_____

_____

_____

Change: Challenging Years of Adolescence _____

_____

_____

_____

Continued on next page

87

Another Look at Adolescence

What's *Right* about Adolescence?
Selected Scripture

Adolescence resembles a house on moving day: it's a mess, but it's a temporary one.

A teenager's life is one that's spent in transit, going somewhere else to be unpacked. And to complicate the move, the hormones are kicking out the slats of the moving crates.

Adolescence—an uphill road to adulthood. An adventure in moving!

But in spite of the problems in packing and the chuckholes along the way, there are some good things about adolescence. And in today's study we want to answer the question "What's *right* about adolescence?"

I. Positive Traits among Adolescents
On the road to adulthood, adolescents often demonstrate a number of exceptional qualities. Four stand out in particular. First, there is *a willingness to risk*—to abandon what is safe and secure and to relocate into new and unfamiliar territory. Second, there is *a sensitivity to God*—to let His Word take root in their lives, to grow in Christ, and to yield the Spirit's fruit. Third, there is *a commitment to integrity*—to consistently live out their convictions. Fourth, there is *a determination to stand*—to deepen their individual roots and withstand the hurricane-force pressure of their peers.

II. Scriptural Examples of These Traits
Four teenagers in the Bible demonstrate these valuable traits. They are Isaac, Samuel, Josiah, and Daniel.

A. Isaac. Well past their childbearing years, Abraham and Sarah were promised a son. God also promised that through this son, Isaac, He would make a great nation that would be a blessing to the entire earth (Gen. 12:1–3, 17:15–19). But when this promised son became a teenager, God threw Abraham a major league curveball.

> Now it came about after these things, that God tested Abraham, and said to him, "Abraham!" And he said, "Here I am." And He said, "Take now your son, your only son, whom you love, Isaac, and go to the land of Moriah; and offer him there as a burnt offering on one of the mountains of which I will tell you." (22:1–2)

Remarkably, Abraham offered no resistance.

> Abraham took the wood of the burnt offering and laid it on Isaac his son, and he took in his hand the fire and the knife. So the two of them walked on

89

together. And Isaac spoke to Abraham his father and said, "My father!" And he said, "Here I am, my son." And he said, "Behold, the fire and the wood, but where is the lamb for the burnt offering?" And Abraham said, "God will provide for Himself the lamb for the burnt offering, my son." So the two of them walked on together. (vv. 6–8)

Like his father, Isaac was also willing to submit himself to the will of God, however incomprehensible, however inscrutable. It was a step of faith, a risk that could cost him his life. But a risk he calculated as worth taking.

Then they came to the place of which God had told him; and Abraham built the altar there, and arranged the wood, and bound his son Isaac, and laid him on the altar on top of the wood. And Abraham stretched out his hand, and took the knife to slay his son. (vv. 9–10)

The Scriptures call us to emulate Isaac's example in a less dramatic but equally important way.

I urge you therefore, brethren, by the mercies of God, to present your bodies a living and holy sacrifice, acceptable to God, which is your spiritual service of worship. (Rom. 12:1)

God is not concerned so much that we give Him our 10 percent tithe as He is that we give our total lives. He wants us to offer ourselves completely, like Isaac did. To offer our plans and our passions, our dreams and our desires, our talents and our treasures. And to offer them freely. Without reservation. Without restriction. Without regret.

B. Samuel. Placed in Eli's custodial care at an early age, Samuel was raised in a less than ideal home (1 Sam. 1:1–2:36). Eli was a successful priest, but an abysmal parent. His two sons blatantly rebelled, bringing shame to their father and to their priestly profession (2:12–17, 22–25). Samuel, however, stood in bold contrast.

Now the boy Samuel was ministering to the Lord before Eli. And word from the Lord was rare in those days, visions were infrequent. And it happened at that time as Eli was lying down in his place (now his eyesight had begun to grow dim and he could not see well), and the lamp of God had not yet gone out, and Samuel was lying down in the temple of the Lord where the ark of God was. (3:1–3)

As we watch young Samuel, we can see that he was responsive and quick to hear God's word.

Then the Lord came and stood and called as at other times, "Samuel! Samuel!" And Samuel said, "Speak, for Thy servant is listening." (v. 10)

With a little help from Eli, Samuel cultivated this quality in his youth. As a result, when he matured he was still responsive and sensitive to God.

Thus Samuel grew and the Lord was with him and let none of his words fail. And all Israel from Dan even to Beersheba knew that Samuel was confirmed as a prophet of the Lord. And the Lord appeared again at Shiloh, because the Lord revealed Himself to Samuel at Shiloh by the word of the Lord. (vv. 19–21)

Hazards of the Move

To be sensitive and submissive to God's voice are two childhood traits that should be stamped FRAGILE.

En route to adulthood, it's easy for these qualities to become dented or broken as they travel over the uncertain road of adolescence. And often, when we finally reach maturity, those are the boxes that are inadvertently left behind or somehow lost in transit.

As your child traffics through the teenage years, put a little extra padding around those two boxes, and be sure to mark them HANDLE WITH CARE.

C. Josiah. Prior to Josiah's reign, leadership was at low tide in Judah. Manasseh reigned fifty-five years and "did evil in the sight of the Lord" (2 Chron. 33:1–9). His son Amon succeeded him and followed the same corrupt path (vv. 21–23). After Amon was assassinated, his young son Josiah was placed on the throne (vv. 24–25). But Josiah did not practice idolatry or immorality as did his predecessors. Instead, he committed himself to integrity. Although we studied his life in the last lesson, let's take a quick review of his character.

Josiah was eight years old when he became king, and he reigned thirty-one years in Jerusalem. And he did right in the sight of the Lord, and walked in the ways of his father David and did not turn aside to the right or to the left. For in the eighth year of his reign while he was still a youth, he began to seek the God of his father David; and in the twelfth year he began to purge Judah and Jerusalem of the high places, the Asherim, the carved images, and the molten images. And they tore down the altars of the Baals in his

91

presence, and the incense altars that were high above them he chopped down; also the Asherim, the carved images, and the molten images he broke in pieces and ground to powder and scattered it on the graves of those who had sacrificed to them. Then he burned the bones of the priests on their altars, and purged Judah and Jerusalem. (34:1–5)

And the fires of this cathartic purge were fanned from the flames of his passion for God—a passion that ignited when he was just sixteen.

D. **Daniel.** Another teenager whose character exemplified something right about adolescence was Daniel. Remember his story from the previous lesson? In the Babylonian captivity, Judah was deported and taken into bondage by King Nebuchadnezzar (Dan. 1:1–2). But the king took a handful of Israel's brightest teenagers and gave them an intensive, three-year crash course on Babylonian culture (vv. 3–5). Part of the indoctrination was culinary, but some of the food was in violation of the Mosaic dietary regulations. It was on this issue that Daniel was determined to take a stand.

But Daniel made up his mind that he would not defile himself with the king's choice food or with the wine which he drank; so he sought permission from the commander of the officials that he might not defile himself. (v. 8)

It was a gutsy stand—a stand which helped put gristle in his spiritual life. And it was a stand that would help give him the courage to step into the lions' den (see chap. 6).

A Thought for the Road

The four teenagers we've studied today exhibit extraordinary qualities of spiritual maturity. They demonstrate that the move from adolescence to adulthood doesn't have to scratch and dent the character en route. Paul's words to the young pastor Timothy leave us with a few tips to ensure safe passage.

Let no one look down on your youthfulness, but rather in speech, conduct, love, faith and purity, show yourself an example of those who believe. (1 Tim. 4:12)

 *Living Insights*

The subject of Old Testament adolescents makes for pretty exciting drama! Let's take one of those cast members and do a more detailed character sketch of his life.

- Choose one of the four teenagers we've just studied who interests you most. Locate the Scriptures that tell of his life and write down your observations.

Further Observations on Adolescence

_____

_____

_____

_____

_____

_____

_____

_____

_____

_____

_____

_____

_____

_____

_____

_____

_____

_____

Living Insights

Mom or Dad, it's easy to see what's *wrong* about your teenagers . . . but take some time to look at what's *right* about them.

- Describe what's right about your adolescent. If you have more than one teenager, write about each of them individually. To make this exercise even more special, why not plan on giving them a copy of what you write!

_____

_____

_____

_____

_____

_____

_____

_____

_____

_____

_____

_____

_____

_____

_____

_____

_____

_____

_____

_____

You and Your Son

Selected Proverbs

Near the end of the nineteenth century, on the heels of a bloody civil war, Josiah Holland wrote:

God, give us men! A time like this demands
Strong minds, great hearts, true faith and ready hands.[1]

God, give us men. Give us Noahs, to whom You can entrust Your mighty plans; give us Abrahams, who are willing to leave home and homeland to follow Your call; give us Josephs, who would rather endure prison than violate one of Your commands; give us Daniels, who would rather face a lions' den than compromise their faith; *God give us men.*

However, before God gives us men, He gives us boys—boys that parents are to forge into men. To help equip parents for that task, God has provided the book of Proverbs, which is largely the advice of a father to his son.

I. Five Areas of Teaching

From Solomon's advice we can glean five areas of teaching that are essential to our sons growing up to be men of God.

A. Teach him to stand alone. Proverbs 1:10–16 accents the need to teach our sons the importance of standing up for biblical convictions, even when that means standing alone.

My son, if sinners entice you,
Do not consent.
If they say, "Come with us,
Let us lie in wait for blood,
Let us ambush the innocent without cause;
Let us swallow them alive like Sheol,[2]
Even whole, as those who go down to the pit;
We shall find all kinds of precious wealth,
We shall fill our houses with spoil;

This lesson is a revised version of "You and Your Son," from the study guide *You and Your Child,* coauthored by Ken Gire, from the Bible-teaching ministry of Charles R. Swindoll (Fullerton, Calif.: Insight for Living, 1986).

1. Josiah Gilbert Holland, "God, Give Us Men!" in *The Best Loved Poems of the American People,* selected by Hazel Felleman (Garden City, N.Y.: Garden City Publishing Co., 1936), p. 132.

2. *Sheol* is "a Hebrew proper noun . . . with a relatively wide range of meanings (mainly 'death,' 'the grave,' 'hell,' 'the next world,' 'the nether world'), making it difficult to determine which of its meanings is in view in any given [Old Testament] passage. . . . It is a place of confinement away from the land of the living. . . . Its use in poetic passages . . . , metaphors, and allegories . . . must be carefully evaluated to differentiate figurative or emotive usages from genuinely descriptive ones." From *The International Standard Bible Encyclopedia,* rev. ed., Geoffrey W. Bromiley, gen. ed. (Grand Rapids, Mich.: William B. Eerdmans Publishing Co., 1988), vol. 4, p. 472.

Throw in your lot with us,
We shall all have one purse,"
My son, do not walk in the way with them.
Keep your feet from their path,
For their feet run to evil,
And they hasten to shed blood.

Notice the three commands: *Do not consent* (v. 10), *do not walk in [their] way* (v. 15), and *keep your feet from their path* (v. 15). Solomon is saying that if the crowd strays from God's path, then follow the path and not the crowd—even if that means walking the path alone. Your child's peer group exerts relentless pressure to conform. So, if pointing out the right path isn't enough, perhaps a change in peer groups is necessary.

He who walks with wise men will be wise,
But the companion of fools will suffer harm. (13:20)

Standing Alone in the Group

Moldy bread has a way of spreading its degenerative spores to all the other slices in the loaf—especially when they're bunched together in the hothouse of a plastic bread bag. So, too, your son's companions can have an unbelievable impact on him. As a rule, we become like the people we spend time with.

If your son seems to have fallen in with a moldy group of friends, how do you encourage him to take the painful step of finding new friends?

First, teach him the qualities of a good friend. As you do this, have him evaluate his current friendships as well as consider the type of friends he would like to have. Remember, though, that forbidding him to associate with certain friends may very well drive him to them. He must ultimately decide for himself.

Second, remind him of the consequences of wrong. Psalm 73 teaches us not to envy wrongdoers but to consider the consequences of their actions (vv. 2–3, 17–20). For children to withstand the magnetic pull of their peer group, it's essential for us to show them the end result of wrong behavior.

B. Teach him to be open to God's counsel. Along with the ability to stand alone, our sons need to be open to God's counsel and reproof. Proverbs 3:11–12 talks about this sensitivity to instruction.

My son, do not reject the discipline of the Lord,
Or loathe His reproof,
For whom the Lord loves He reproves,
Even as a father, the son in whom he delights.

A tender heart toward God is one of the hallmarks of manhood. David, the great warrior and king, was as fierce as "a bear robbed of her cubs" (2 Sam. 17:8). Yet he was also described as a man after God's heart, seeking to do His will (Acts 13:22). David was open to God's counsel.

A Sensitive Spirit

How do you develop sensitivity in the life of your son? First of all, teach him how to respond to *your* counsel (see Prov. 1:8–9, 2:1–5, 3:1–4, 4:1–5, 5:1, 7:1–3). If he treasures your counsel, it will be an easier transition to treasure God's counsel.

Second, help him see the value of other people's correction. If he learns to respect the reproof of his teacher, coach, employer, and others around him, he will naturally grow to respect God's correction.

Third, share your life with him. Tell him about both the positive and negative experiences you've had, and what you've learned from them.

Fourth, spend sufficient time counseling your son. Remember, you're not molding a tin soldier for the dime store—you're forging a great man for God! And that takes time.

C. **Teach him how to deal with temptation.** Proverbs primarily mentions two areas of temptation—the enticement of the opposite sex and the excessive use of food and drink.

   1. **Sexual temptation.** Look at what Proverbs 5:1–6 says with regard to sexual temptation.

   My son, give attention to my wisdom ...
   The lips of an adulteress drip honey,
   And smoother than oil is her speech;
   But in the end she is bitter as wormwood,
   Sharp as a two-edged sword.
   Her feet go down to death,
   Her steps lay hold of Sheol.
   She does not ponder the path of life;
   Her ways are unstable, she does not know it.

   These powerful words tell us there are real dangers in tasting the forbidden fruit of sexual relationships outside marriage. And parents must explain these dangers, while extolling the Edenic beauty of romantic marital love (see vv. 15–19, Song of Solomon). As in Eden, temptation ultimately comes from the center of the garden—our heart (Matt. 5:28; compare James 1:13–14). Whether your son is a victor or victim of lust is determined daily on the battlefield of his heart. Furthermore, your son needs to realize that overcoming temptation is a continual battle (see Rom. 6–8).

2. **Excessive indulgence.** Proverbs has some equally pointed advice with regard to food and drink.

> Listen, my son, and be wise,
> And direct your heart in the way.
> Do not be with heavy drinkers of wine,
> Or with gluttonous eaters of meat;
> For the heavy drinker and the glutton will come
>   to poverty,
> And drowsiness will clothe a man with rags.
> (23:19–21)

If we become pleasure's slave, it becomes a harsh, exacting taskmaster (see vv. 29–35).

D. Teach him how to handle money. The subject of finances covers four areas: teaching your son how to give, earn, spend, and save.[3]

1. **Giving.** He should learn to honor the Lord with his income by making giving his first priority (3:9–10), especially giving to the poor (22:9).

2. **Earning.** In order to give, he must learn some skill with which he can derive an income (Eph. 4:28, 1 Thess. 4:11, 2 Thess. 3:6–12).

3. **Spending.** The woman in Proverbs 31 exemplifies how to wisely spend and invest money (see especially vv. 14, 16, 21, 24; compare Matt. 25:14–30).

4. **Saving.** The principle of saving is best seen in Solomon's illustration of the ant who stored food in the summer so she could eat in the winter (Prov. 6:6–8).

E. Teach him the value of hard work. Two more passages from Proverbs underscore the value of hard work.

> Poor is he who works with a negligent hand,
> But the hand of the diligent makes rich.
> He who gathers in summer is a son who acts wisely,

---

3. An excellent resource for teaching your children how to handle money is *Money Matters for Parents and Their Kids,* by Ron and Judy Blue (Nashville, Tenn.: Thomas Nelson Publishers, 1988).

But he who sleeps in harvest is a son who acts
shamefully....
The soul of the sluggard craves and gets nothing,
But the soul of the diligent is made fat.
(10:4–5, 13:4)

In a nutshell, hard work pays off. Hard, diligent work also pays off in raising your son. After years of planting, watering, weeding, nourishing, and waiting, the harvest of your diligence will be evident in your relationship with your son. And if you have led him to walk with God's Son, your barns will then be truly full, and your riches will be eternal.

II. Two Added Ingredients

As you teach your son to be a man of God, you'll need two additional ingredients: *constant delight* and *consistent discipline.* While your son must learn the value of the rod, he must always know that you love him and delight in him, for "love covers all transgressions" (10:12).

The Best Teacher

More than your words, your example—how *you* handle convictions, counsel, temptation, money, and work—will be your son's most convincing teacher.

 Living Insights

Study One ■━━━━━━━━━━━━━━━━━━━━━━━━━━━━━━━━━━━━━━━

The word *son* or *sons* is mentioned over forty times in the book of Proverbs. Let's take a look at some of these references.

● The following list gives twelve verses that include the word *son* or *sons.* Look up each verse and jot down a few words of summary. As you write, allow the truth of each passage to sink in.

Proverbs about Sons

1:8 _____

_____

3:1 _____

_____

Continued on next page

3:11 _____

_____

4:10 _____

_____

10:1 _____

_____

13:1 _____

_____

13:24 _____

_____

19:27 _____

_____

20:7 _____

_____

23:15 _____

_____

28:7 _____

_____

29:17 _____

_____

 Living Insights

Study Two ▬▬▬▬▬▬▬▬▬▬▬▬▬▬▬▬▬▬▬▬▬▬▬

Our children are our legacy. As a parent, are you taking that thought seriously? If you have a young son, take some time to review and apply today's lesson.

- Below are the five areas of training from our study. Rate yourself in regard to how you communicate these to your son, with 5 being highest.

Standing Alone	1	2	3	4	5
Being Open to God's Counsel	1	2	3	4	5
Dealing with Temptation	1	2	3	4	5
Handling Finances	1	2	3	4	5
Working Hard	1	2	3	4	5

Take time to develop an action plan that would improve any weak areas.

_____

_____

_____

_____

_____

_____

_____

- Now rate yourself on the two added ingredients for successfully parenting your son.

Constant Delight	1	2	3	4	5
Consistent Discipline	1	2	3	4	5

How will you ensure that these qualities remain balanced?

_____

_____

_____

_____

You and Your Daughter
(Part One)
Selected Proverbs

Gone With the Wind, Margaret Mitchell's first and only novel, stands a classic, both as a book and as a film. The backdrop to the story is the war-torn South. But it's not a story about the Civil War. It's a story about one woman—Scarlett O'Hara—a ravishing woman men hover over like flies around a watermelon. But under the coy twirl of the parasol that shades her fine-china skin; beneath her honeyed, rose-petal lips; behind the flirtatious flutter of her inviting eyes, there hides a woman whose heart is "snares and nets" (Eccles. 7:26).

As a contrast, the author continually places Scarlett beside the kind, pure, accepting Melanie. Next to Melanie, Scarlett is seen for what she really is—a conniving, manipulative, ruthless woman.

In similar style, Proverbs often compares and contrasts its characters. Today we will compare and contrast two sets of women and, in doing so, learn qualities that can help our daughters become godly women.

I. Wise Woman and Foolish
Consider the two women in Proverbs 14:1.
The wise woman builds her house,
But the foolish tears it down with her own hands.
Literally, the Hebrew word for *foolish* means "dull, thick, sluggish."[1] The foolish woman of this verse is dulled to wisdom, calloused to correction, and sluggish in her response to God. Destruction lies in the wake of every wave she makes. The phrase *tears down* comes from a single Hebrew word meaning "to overthrow, to destroy." Conversation by conversation, circumstance by circumstance, relationship by relationship, she dismantles her house one board at a time. Her guilt is underscored by the phrase *with her own hands.* Finally, after years of troubling her own house, she will only "inherit wind" (11:29a). No parents want their daughter's life to turn out like that. But what most parents don't realize is that the foolish woman of Proverbs 14 started out as a foolish daughter—a daughter whose foolishness was never fully recognized or effectively dealt with. Let's look at some diagnostic X rays of a foolish woman. They will help

This lesson is a revised version of "You and Your Daughter" (Part One), from the study guide *You and Your Child,* coauthored by Ken Gire, from the Bible-teaching ministry of Charles R. Swindoll (Fullerton, Calif.: Insight for Living, 1986).

1. A portrait of a fool can be found in Derek Kidner's *The Proverbs* (Downers Grove, Ill.: InterVarsity Press, 1964), pp. 39–41.

you determine whether the condition exists in your daughter and how you can catch the malignancy before it proves fatal.

A. Symptoms of foolishness. Proverbs reveals four qualities of a foolish woman.

1. **She is boisterous.** Notice this first symptom in 9:13.

   The woman of folly is boisterous,
   She is naive, and knows nothing.

   By *boisterous,* the text doesn't mean energetic or excitable. Rather, the thought is one of commotion and turbulence.[2] Picture an electric mixer whirling batter all over the kitchen or a dust storm spinning through your house, and you get something of the idea.

2. **She makes a mockery of sin.** Proverbs 14:9a states: "Fools mock at sin." The foolish woman of chapter 9 illustrates this in her making light of adultery.

   "Stolen water is sweet;
   And bread eaten in secret is pleasant." (v. 17)

   Her seared conscience is insensitive to sin, causing her to flippantly indulge in its passing pleasures. Right and wrong are not important to her; only what is sweet and pleasant. Her focus on a live-for-the-moment lifestyle is short-sighted and blurs her eyes to the long-term effects of her actions— thus validating that she is truly "naive, and knows nothing."

3. **She is deceptive.** Proverbs 14:8b tells us that "the folly of fools is deceit." She can look you eyeball-to-eyeball and, without batting a lash, deceive you in the most convincing way.

4. **She is quarrelsome.** A final symptom of foolishness appears in 20:3.

   Keeping away from strife is an honor for a man,
   But any fool will quarrel.

   The Hebrew term translated *quarrel* means "to burst forth in a rage, a tantrum." A foolish daughter is argumentative and given to rage.

A Look Inside

Put your daughter behind the X-ray machine for a moment. Now take a good, hard look. What do you see?

Is she in a constant state of turbulence, filled with uneasiness and commotion? Does she treat sin lightly

---

2. "This root, used thirty-four times, means 'cry out,' 'make a loud noise,' or 'be turbulent.' It is a strong word, emphasizing unrest, commotion, strong feeling, or noise." *Theological Wordbook of the Old Testament,* ed. R. Laird Harris, Gleason L. Archer, Jr., and Bruce K. Waltke (Chicago, Ill.: Moody Press, 1980), vol. 1, p. 219.

and flippantly? Is she deceptive and given to lying? Is she quarrelsome and argumentative? If you see these symptoms in your daughter now, the prognosis for her future is not good. In fact, we say with a surgeon's frankness, her future holds only heartache and tragedy. If you are the parent of a foolish child, your future is no brighter.

He who begets a fool does so to his sorrow,
And the father of a fool has no joy. (17:21)

Furthermore, you will be raising a Scarlett whose house will be troubled, torn down, and literally gone with the wind. But if you catch the foolishness early enough and confront it with the combination of a physician's decisiveness, firmness, and tenderness, then you can grace the world with a Melanie—a wise woman who "builds her house."

B. Attributes of wisdom. How, then, do parents raise daughters to be wise, godly women? Proverbs 31 gives us five areas on which to concentrate.
  1. **Help her realize the value of being wise.**
       An excellent wife, who can find?
       For her worth is far above jewels. . . .
       She opens her mouth in wisdom,
       And the teaching of kindness is on her tongue.
       (vv. 10, 26)
     When she realizes that wisdom is more precious than jewels (see 3:13–15), she will have taken the first step toward gaining that wisdom.
  2. **Develop in her a spirit of submission.** A wise woman has a servant's heart, using her life to build up others.
       The heart of her husband trusts in her,
       And he will have no lack of gain.
       She does him good and not evil
       All the days of her life. (31:11–12)
     Your daughter is more likely to develop a submissive spirit if she sees the submissive spirit of Christ incarnate in your everyday life (compare Phil. 2:3–8, Mark 10:45).
  3. **Teach her the skills of her hands.** This is the tangible expression of wisdom that imparts practical skills for daily living.
       She looks for wool and flax,
       And works with her hands in delight. (Prov. 31:13)

104

4. **Teach her how to handle money.** Just as you teach your son about money, so you need to instill sound financial wisdom in your daughter. As a family, learn some wise ways to spend and save.

She considers a field and buys it;
From her earnings she plants a vineyard. (v. 16)

5. **Teach her the blessings of hard work** (see vv. 17–24). Because a wise woman is not afraid to work,

Strength and dignity are her clothing,
And she smiles at the future. (v. 25)

Now that's what you want for your daughter, isn't it? By applying these five principles to your parenting, you will see your daughter develop strength and dignity . . . and a future to smile at.

II. Contentious Woman and Gracious

Proverbs paints a vivid portrait of a contentious woman.

The contentions of a wife are a constant dripping. (19:13b)

It is better to live in a corner of a roof,
Than in a house shared with a contentious woman. (21:9)

It is better to live in a desert land,
Than with a contentious and vexing woman. (v. 19)

A constant dripping on a day of steady rain
And a contentious woman are alike;
He who would restrain her restrains the wind,
And grasps oil with his right hand. (27:15–16)

What images do you see in this picture? First, a leaky faucet. If you've ever had one keep you awake at night, you understand. Second, the corner of a roof. If you've ever been on your roof to fix an antenna, you know things would have to be pretty bad to consider living there. Third, a desert. Blistering, relentless sun—doesn't sound too inviting. Fourth, constant dripping on a rainy day. Nag, nag, nag, nag, nag—even sounds like dripping rain, doesn't it? And fifth, slippery oil. Try to grab hold of it sometime—it will drive you crazy. All these images picture a woman given to strife. She thrives on stirring up hornets' nests. And she always manages to get in the last word. Like a continual drip . . . drip . . . drip, she drives you up a wall and out the window.

A Look in the Mirror

I'll try to wrap this brick in velvet, but the hard truth is, many contentious daughters are that way because they have contentious mothers.

Now wait! Before you throw the brick back—remember, like begets like. We *do* reproduce after our kind. Pick up the mirror of James 1:19. What do you see? A person who is "quick to hear, slow to speak and slow to anger"? Look harder. Is that you? Because if you're slow to hear, quick to speak, and quick to anger—you're looking a lot like a contentious woman. And guess who will mirror that image? Yes—your daughter. Fortunately, the mirror has another side—the woman of Proverbs 11: "A gracious woman attains honor" (v. 16a).

To be gracious means "to show favor." A gracious person is accepting and appreciative. A woman shows her graciousness through her speech, her appearance, and her response to authority. Mirror graciousness to your daughter clearly and consistently, and glimpse by glimpse she will become a changed person. And someday, she will attain honor as a gracious woman.

 Living Insights

Study One

The most famous biblical description of a godly woman is found in the last chapter of Proverbs. Let's look again at this passage.

● Earlier we used the technique of paraphrasing. Let's once again tap into this vital resource for personal Bible study. Take Proverbs 31:10–31 and put the twenty-two verses into your own words. Work hard to allow your paraphrase to reflect your own understanding of each phrase.

Continued on next page

 *Living Insights*

In our last study, we worked through Proverbs 31:10–31. Now it's time to make it personal.

- In the following chart, list ten qualities you admire most from the Proverbs 31 description of a wise and gracious woman. Next to them, list the verses in which you find these qualities. If you are a woman, use the third column to give yourself a personal evaluation for each quality. Be honest and objective. If you're a man, think of the woman closest to you (wife, daughter, mother, or friend) and place a check (✔) next to the traits she best demonstrates. Make an opportunity to communicate this to her . . . soon!

A Woman of God			
Qualities You Admire	Verses	Personal Evaluation	✔

You and Your Daughter
(Part Two)
Selected Proverbs

In one of her many books about family life, Dale Evans Rogers quotes this tender tribute to a daughter, titled "What Is a Girl?"

"Little girls are the nicest things that happen to people. . . .

"A girl is Innocence playing in the mud, Beauty standing on its head, and Motherhood dragging a doll by the foot. . . .

"God borrows from many creatures to make a girl. He uses the song of the bird, the squeal of a pig, the stubbornness of the mule, the antics of a monkey, the spryness of a grasshopper, the curiosity of a cat, the speed of a gazelle, the slyness of a fox, the softness of a kitten. . . .

". . . She is the loudest when you are thinking, the prettiest when she has provoked you, the busiest at bedtime, the quietest when you want to show her off, and the most flirtatious when she absolutely must not get the best of you again.

"Who else can cause you more grief, joy, irritation, satisfaction, embarrassment and genuine delight than this combination of Eve, Salome, and Florence Nightingale?" [1]

Some of you with young daughters are probably nodding in agreement as you read this description. Others of you with older daughters may be leaning back in your chair, cynically thinking, "You just wait." For some, raising daughters can be a delight; for others, a disaster. How the experience turns out for you depends on the qualities you are building into your daughter's life right now. As a follow-up to our previous lesson, we'll examine two more contrasting pairs of women: sensuous and virtuous, indiscreet and godly.

I. Sensuous Woman and Virtuous

These days, the sensuous woman rides the crest of a Madison Avenue wave while the virtuous woman sits alone on the beach. But one day that wave will come crashing upon the shoals, and the undercurrent of her illicit actions will sweep the sensuous woman into the depths.

This lesson is a revised version of "You and Your Daughter" (Part Two), from the study guide *You and Your Child*, coauthored by Ken Gire, from the Bible-teaching ministry of Charles R. Swindoll (Fullerton, Calif.: Insight for Living, 1986).

1. Alan Beck, as quoted by Dale Evans Rogers in *Time Out, Ladies!* (Westwood, N.J.: Fleming H. Revell Co., 1966), pp. 55–56.

A. The sensuous woman. Proverbs 2:16 describes the sexually promiscuous woman as *the strange woman*. The term means "estranged, alienated." She is estranged from her family and outside the circle of proper relationships. The following proverbs peel away her smooth veneer and allow us to see her as she really is.

The strange woman,
. . . the adulteress who flatters with her words;
. . . leaves the companion of her youth,
And forgets the covenant of her God;
For her house sinks down to death,
And her tracks lead to the dead;
None who go to her return again,
Nor do they reach the paths of life.
(2:16–19)

The lips of an adulteress drip honey,
And smoother than oil is her speech;
But in the end she is bitter as wormwood,
Sharp as a two-edged sword.
Her feet go down to death,
Her steps lay hold of Sheol.
She does not ponder the path of life;
Her ways are unstable, she does not know it.
(5:3–6)

For the commandment is a lamp, and the teaching
    is light;
And reproofs for discipline are the way of life,
To keep you from the evil woman,
From the smooth tongue of the adulteress.
Do not desire her beauty in your heart,
Nor let her catch you with her eyelids.
For on account of a harlot one is reduced to a loaf
    of bread,
And an adulteress hunts for the precious life.
(6:23–26)

I saw among the naive . . .
A young man lacking sense . . .
And behold, a woman comes to meet him,
Dressed as a harlot and cunning of heart.
She is boisterous and rebellious;
Her feet do not remain at home. . . .
With her many persuasions she entices him;
With her flattering lips she seduces him.

Suddenly he follows her . . .
[And] he does not know that it will cost him his life.
(7:7, 10–11, 21–22a, 23b)
Your daughter may never run off into the barren wilderness of sexual promiscuity. However, she may be wandering precariously close to its borders if you can see qualities of Proverbs' strange woman emerging in her.

A Word to Fathers of Daughters

Take the preceding composite of the adulterous woman and place it beside a picture of your daughter. See any similarities? Is your daughter overly interested in external beauty? Does the way she dress hint at seduction? Listen to your daughter's conversations. Is she given to verbal flattery? Do her words entice or persuade? Examine her attitudes. Is she rebellious? Does she hate to be at home, taking every opportunity to get out of the house? If so, take these warning signs to heart and plan some positive steps.

A growing daughter needs warmth, affection, and communication—especially from her father. She needs smiles and hugs and reassurances of your love. She needs candid talks about life, about what a man looks for in a woman, and about what the Bible says concerning inner and outer beauty.

Fathers, you can lose your daughters by default, simply by not being there—or if there, by being silent and passive. Instead of taking a step back from her, take a step toward her—and give her the biggest hug, the warmest smile, and the most sincere "I love you" that you possibly can. Assure her of your love often enough so those messages will start transforming her from the inside out.

B. The virtuous woman. In Hebrew, the word *virtuous* means "firm, strong, efficient, able" and conveys a sense of moral worth. Proverbs 31:10–31 describes this woman of God as a jewel of a wife. This passage holds her high in the shimmering light to shine as the perfect role model for every growing girl. The virtuous woman's finely cut facets sparkle brilliantly—she is trustworthy, diligent, committed to the family's well-being, prudent, generous, strong, has integrity, speaks wisely, is kind, and is appreciated by her family. As a life assignment, begin using Proverbs 31:10–31 as a prayer list for your daughter. It's the best way to begin to get a diamond in the rough out of the rough!

II. Indiscreet Woman and Godly

As we'll learn in this final comparison of two women, beauty is, indeed, only skin deep.

A. The indiscreet woman. A woman with discretion is praised (1 Sam. 25:32–33), while a woman without discretion is depicted in ridiculous terms.

> As a ring of gold in a swine's snout,
> So is a beautiful woman who lacks discretion.
> (Prov. 11:22)

The word *discretion* comes from the Hebrew word meaning "to taste" and carries the idea of discriminating taste (see Ps. 34:8).[2] It is the ability to choose between the tasteful and the tasteless, the appropriate and the inappropriate, right and wrong, good and bad. A woman lacking that ability, no matter how beautiful, becomes as repulsive as the runny snout of a pig. And her outward beauty, like the gold ring, is totally out of harmony with her inner self.

B. The godly woman. A more pleasing image is the woman of discretion in Proverbs 31, who is in harmony with her inner self.

> Charm is deceitful and beauty is vain,
> But a woman who fears the Lord, she shall be praised.
> (v. 30)

The woman who fears the Lord realizes that charm can conceal the truth of a woman's character and beauty can mask an empty life. She discriminates between the eternal and the temporal and places the appropriate value on each.

Whispered Words of Wisdom

First Peter 3:3–4 provides some excellent advice to every young woman.

> Let not your adornment be merely external— braiding the hair, and wearing gold jewelry, or putting on dresses; but let it be the hidden person of the heart, with the imperishable quality of a gentle and quiet spirit, which is precious in the sight of God.

Like all of us, your daughter is constantly being bombarded with messages from our culture that say physical beauty is everything for a woman. Almost every magazine,

---

2. "The primary meaning of the root is 'to try, or to evaluate, with the tongue, normally with a view to consumption if the flavor is suitable.'" *Theological Wordbook of the Old Testament,* ed. R. Laird Harris, Gleason L. Archer, Jr., and Bruce K. Waltke (Chicago, Ill.: Moody Press, 1980), vol. 1, p. 351.

every commercial, every billboard, every movie communicates that message, either explicitly or implicitly. And unless you get close enough to your daughter to whisper what is precious in God's sight, she may never get the true message.

 Living Insights

Study One ▬▬▬▬▬▬▬▬▬▬▬▬▬▬▬

In "You and Your Daughter" (Part One) we used our Living Insights to examine the characteristics of the excellent woman of Proverbs 31. But many times we can learn even more by providing a point of contrast. Because if we understand the lifestyle of the sensuous woman, we can better appreciate the qualities of the excellent woman.

• The following five passages list character traits of the sensuous woman. Write these traits in the middle column; then refer to the previous lesson's chart on the excellent woman to identify some points of contrast.

The Sensuous Woman		
Proverbs	Character Traits	Contrasts
2:16–19		
5:3–6		
6:23–26		
7:6–27		
9:13–18		

113

Living Insights

This next assignment should give you some real living insights into your daughter!

Ask her to go out for a special evening with you—dinner, entertainment, the works. Be creative, and go out of your way to make it relaxed, memorable, and *fun*. No lectures. No correction. No parent-to-child talks. Nothing heavy or intimidating.

For one evening, forget you're an adult, and try to get into her world. Music and movies are generally common ground for most children. Try not to pass judgment or offer any unsolicited opinions. Instead, just listen and try to gain a broader understanding of your daughter and her world.

It would be a treat for her if you shared what you were like when you were her age—how you felt about dating, your worst date, your best date, what movies and music were popular then, how you felt about growing up, how you felt about your parents, and so forth. Tailor the evening to her age and her interests.

Make it a scrapbook memory for her—and for you too—one you both will treasure for a lifetime.

Section Four:

WISDOM CLAIMED WHILE WEATHERING THE STORMS

Releasing the Reins

Ephesians 4:11–16

Of all God's creatures, humans have the hardest time releasing their offspring. Bears have no trouble saying good-bye to their cubs. Wolves don't slump into depression once their litter is weaned and leaves home. And eagles literally push their eaglets out of the nest.

So why do humans instinctively want to hold on to their children? Why do we take so long to release the reins? Why do we try to keep our children in the nest when they should be out flying on their own?

Maybe we fear they're not quite ready for the real world. Maybe we feel we haven't done an adequate job of preparing them to face life. Unfortunately, keeping them in the nest offers no assurance that they will develop stronger wings. In fact, children who are coddled too long in the nest often never develop the strength to fly on their own. They grow into adults who lack self-confidence and the ability to think and act independently.

Releasing the reins allows children the opportunity to stretch their *own* wings. It is difficult to sit back and watch them leave, perched precariously on the edge of the nest, wings fluttering uncertainly. But that time of departure can be easier if we understand the process.

I. Progressive Cycles in Families

The first step in preparing to release your child is to understand the cycles that most families go through. Like the seasons, these stages overlap to a certain degree and vary in length, but basically they follow a definite progression.

Stage one: Family founding. This begins with the wedding and goes through the birth of the first child.

Stage two: Childbearing. This starts with the birth of the first child and lasts until the last child enters school.

115

Stage three: Child rearing. This lasts from the time the first child enters school until the last child enters college or leaves home.

Stage four: Child launching. Beginning with the first child's departure from home, this stage lasts until the last child leaves.

Stage five: Empty nest. All the children have left home now.

Each of these stages has its own struggles, but perhaps none is so heartrending as the fourth. Mothers who have wrapped their entire lives around their children sometimes become devastated when their children leave home. Fathers who have smothered their children with control sometimes become resentful when their authority is eclipsed by their children's independent steps toward freedom. But launching children from the nest needn't be a traumatic experience if certain principles are taken into consideration.

II. Preparation and Principles for Child Launching

In Ephesians 4, the primary application deals with the growth and development of our heavenly family—the church. However, we can also apply the principles to the growth and development of our earthly families. Verses 11–12 describe the role and responsibility of those special leaders in God's family.

And He gave some as apostles, and some as prophets, and some as evangelists, and some as pastors and teachers, for the equipping of the saints for the work of service, to the building up of the body of Christ.

Just as God appointed leaders for the church, so He has designated parents to lead the family. Their job description? To equip and build up their children so they might successfully survive the seasons of life. Here are some principles that will help prepare your children—and you—for that time of release.

A. Principle one: Keep your role uppermost in mind.

Equipping children for life is your role—not keeping them near your side. You are to prepare them for adult life, as church leaders prepare their members.

For the equipping of the saints for the work of service, to the building up of the body of Christ; until we all attain to the unity of the faith, and of the knowledge of the Son of God, to a mature man, to the measure of the stature which belongs to the fulness of Christ. (vv. 12–13)

Ultimately, church members must be loyal not to their leaders but to the Lord. This is also true of the parent-child relationship. Verse 12 describes the process of equipping, which leads to service, which, in turn, leads to the overall health and growth of the body of Christ. In this process parents, like church leaders, can know they're on the right track when they see their children growing in unity, increasing in the knowledge of God, becoming mature, and incarnating the character of Christ.

B. Principle two: Watch for signs of maturity and reward the result. Maturity unfolds at a different rate and fashion with each child. Like the blooming of a flower, it shouldn't be forced. However, as each petal of maturity unfurls itself, parents should recognize the progress and reward it appropriately. On the road to maturity, our children may take an occasional detour or hit a chuckhole. When that happens, we, as parents, need to be there . . . to guide, to encourage, and to help them find their way.

> As a result, we are no longer to be children, tossed here and there by waves, and carried about by every wind of doctrine, by the trickery of men, by craftiness in deceitful scheming; but speaking the truth in love, we are to grow up in all aspects into Him, who is the head, even Christ. (vv. 14–15)

Love doesn't stand at the side of the road in silence. Nor does it shout, "I told you so!" Instead, love speaks the truth, in a constructive and gentle manner.

C. Principle three: When an older child reverts to childishness, confront the behavior with honesty and love. The Bible doesn't take a sink-or-swim approach to parenting. Parents aren't supposed to stand on the riverbank passively watching their children wade into deep and treacherous waters. Instead, we should follow Proverbs 27:5–6, which gives some helpful advice for what we should do when our children make mistakes.

> Better is open rebuke
> Than love that is concealed.
> Faithful are the wounds of a friend,
> But deceitful are the kisses of an enemy.

D. Principle four: Help your children discover and develop their own individuality, respecting it in a context of love. Turning our attention again to Ephesians 4, we note that each and every member of Christ's body is unique and important.

> The whole body, being fitted and held together by that which every joint supplies, according to the proper working of each individual part, causes the growth of the body for the building up of itself in love. (v. 16)

When you treat your children as individuals, uniquely crafted by God for a special place in the body of Christ and in society, their sense of self-worth is enhanced. They then can see themselves as "fearfully and wonderfully made" instead of mass-manufactured on some celestial assembly line.

III. Two Rules to Remember

As we conclude this subject of releasing the reins, a couple of rules will help us let go.

A. Encourage growth rather than tolerate it. Growth is an evidence of life. Continued growth produces both maturity and stability, two qualities David prayed about for his children.

Let our sons in their youth be as grown-up plants,
And our daughters as corner pillars fashioned as for
a palace. (Ps. 144:12)

B. Release continually, not suddenly. Every year, release your grip a little bit more. In fact, you should begin releasing as soon as they are born. Remember, God has loaned your children to you for just a few years. They are borrowed treasure, not owned. You are trustees of that treasure, not titleholders. And when releasing your child seems an emotionally exhausting task, remember that God the Father set the example—releasing His only Son from the nest of heaven into a hostile world.

 Living Insights

Study One ▬▬▬▬▬▬▬▬▬▬▬▬▬▬▬▬▬▬▬▬▬▬▬▬▬▬

One of the beauties of God's Word is its breadth. Paul addressed Ephesians 4 primarily to God's family—the church. Yet its emphasis applies equally to our earthly families—our Christian homes.

• By now you're familiar with the art of paraphrasing. Try your hand at writing Ephesians 4:11–16 in your own words. For even greater application, paraphrase it with your earthly family in mind. Bring out the meanings and feelings underneath the words in this marvelous passage.

_____

_____

_____

_____

_____

_____

_____

_____

_____

_____

_____

_____

_____

_____

_____

Living Insights

Study Two ▬▬▬▬▬▬▬▬▬▬▬▬▬▬▬▬▬▬▬

Learning to release the reins is a necessity. For some, this is a review; for others, a preview; for the rest, a reflection of what they're encountering this very moment. Where are you?

- Let's use our Living Insights today as a time for self-evaluation. Choose one of the following headings that most appropriately fits your family situation and jot down your thoughts.

Releasing the Reins: How I Did It

_____

_____

_____

_____

_____

_____

_____

_____

Continued on next page

119

Releasing the Reins: How I'm Doing It

_____

_____

_____

_____

_____

_____

_____

_____

Releasing the Reins: How I Will Do It

_____

_____

_____

_____

_____

_____

_____

What about the Older Rebel?
Luke 15:11–24

The pain of having a prodigal child. Can any pain be more disorienting for a parent? More defeating? More devastating? What do you do when a child is too stubborn to listen? Too angry to reason with? Too old to spank?

John White, in his excellent book *Parents in Pain,* provides a biblical answer.

God's dealings with his people form a pattern for Christian parents. Like him we may eventually have to allow our persistently rebellious children to harvest the consequences of their willfulness. The time can come when we have to withdraw all support from them and oblige them, because of their own decisions, to leave home.[1]

Hard words. But as we will see in today's study, they are wise words.

I. God's Response to a Rebellious Will
In the Old Testament era, God took a bold, uncompromising stand on rebellion.

A. An indictment from the Old Testament. Rebellious children were as much a problem in ancient times as they are today. The method of dealing with the problem back then, however, was considerably more decisive and final.

"If any man has a stubborn and rebellious son who will not obey his father or his mother, and when they chastise him, he will not even listen to them, then his father and mother shall seize him, and bring him out to the elders of his city at the gateway of his home town. And they shall say to the elders of his city, 'This son of ours is stubborn and rebellious, he will not obey us, he is a glutton and a drunkard.' Then all the men of his city shall stone him to death; so you shall remove the evil from your midst, and all Israel shall hear of it and fear." (Deut. 21:18–21)

These measures appear brutal and extreme, but God viewed the sin of rebellion as seriously as He did the worship of demons and idols.

---

1. John White, *Parents in Pain* (Downers Grove, Ill.: InterVarsity Press, 1979), p. 201. Used by permission.

"For rebellion is as the sin of divination,
And insubordination is as iniquity and idolatry."
(1 Sam. 15:23a)[2]

B. An illustration from the Old Testament. Though devoted to serving as a priest before God, Eli responded passively to the brash rebellion of his two sons (1 Sam. 2:23–25a). Because of his tolerance, shame was brought not only on his house but on the house of God (vv. 12–17, 22, 29–30). And because Eli didn't face the seriousness of the problem and stop his sons, God stepped in and did it for him.

"In that day I will carry out against Eli all that I have spoken concerning his house, from beginning to end. For I have told him that I am about to judge his house forever for the iniquity which he knew, because his sons brought a curse on themselves and he did not rebuke them." (3:12–13; see also 2:31–36)

The methods of dealing with a rebellious child change from the Old Testament to the New. As we look at the love expressed by the father of the prodigal son, we'll see that it's still an example of tough love, but it is gracious in its means and redemptive in its goal.

II. Christ's Parable of a Rebellious Son

Acclaimed by literary critics as the greatest short story ever written, the parable of the prodigal son is a classic illustration of how to deal with rebellion in a Christlike way.

A. The setting. The story is set in first-century Palestine, but the drama is contemporary, enacted every day across the world.

And [Jesus] said, "A certain man had two sons; and the younger of them said to his father, 'Father, give me the share of the estate that falls to me.' And he divided his wealth between them. And not many days later, the younger son gathered everything together and went on a journey into a distant country." (Luke 15:11–13a)

Jewish law said that when a family had two sons, the eldest would get two-thirds of his father's estate and the youngest

---

2. Opposition to God is the common denominator between rebellion and divination. Rebellion opposes God's authority directly. Divination opposes it indirectly by worshiping forces antagonistic to God. Insubordination is like idolatry in that "all conscious disobedience . . . makes self-will, the human I, into a god. . . . All manifest opposition to the word and commandment of God is, like idolatry, a rejection of the true God." C. F. Keil and F. Delitzsch, *Commentary on the Old Testament* (reprint, Grand Rapids, Mich.: William B. Eerdmans Publishing Co., 1982), vol. 2, p. 157.

would get the remaining third at his father's retirement or death. Given the younger brother's rivalry with his more dutiful, older brother, the prodigal son undoubtedly felt that when his father died the older brother would take the prime pastureland and he would get stuck with the rocky back forty. Because of these tensions at home and because of a craving to see the world, the younger son decided to leave home.

Tough Love

Deciding to let his son leave was probably the most heartrending choice this father ever faced. Yet his love for his son overcame any reluctance he had. Again we turn to John White:

> Parents who are reluctant to take drastic steps should ask themselves why. Are they too scared? There is every reason to be scared. What parent is not? The thought of exposing a child to physical hardship, to loneliness and to moral temptation flies in the face of every parental instinct....
>
> Yet love must respect the dignity, the personhood of the beloved. You cannot love someone truly and deny that person the dignity of facing the results of his or her decisions. To do anything else would be to betray true love for something less than love, a "love" tainted by selfishness and weakness. Paradoxically we cannot love unless we risk the doom of the one we love.[3]

B. The lifestyle. Having slipped off the collar of domestic responsibility, the younger son trotted off to answer the call of the wild, " 'and there he squandered his estate with loose living' " (v. 13b). The prodigal's eat-drink-and-be-merry lifestyle eventually slid him into a moral and financial pigsty.

> "Now when he had spent everything, a severe famine occurred in that country, and he began to be in need. And he went and attached himself to one of the citizens of that country, and he sent him into his fields to feed swine. And he was longing to fill his stomach with the pods that the swine were eating, and no one was giving anything to him." (vv. 14–16)

3. White, *Parents in Pain,* pp. 204, 206. Used by permission.

C. The return. With his funds exhausted, the pleasure seeker became a pauper, caught in the ravenous jaws of a famine. But with the crunch at its worst, he came to his senses. He shook loose from his circumstances and, with his tail between his legs, slinked home.

> "When he came to his senses, he said, 'How many of my father's hired men have more than enough bread, but I am dying here with hunger! I will get up and go to my father, and will say to him, "Father, I have sinned against heaven, and in your sight; I am no longer worthy to be called your son; make me as one of your hired men."' And he got up and came to his father." (vv. 17–20a)

What turned this wayward son's heart toward home? A mental picture of his father...a picture that gains color and depth when we realize that the son never visualized his father turning him away.

D. The response. Verses 20b–24 resemble a climactic scene in an Academy Award-winning film. As you read, feel the emotion, the ecstasy, the tears of joy.

> "But while he was still a long way off, his father saw him, and felt compassion for him, and ran and embraced him, and kissed him. And the son said to him, 'Father, I have sinned against heaven and in your sight; I am no longer worthy to be called your son.' But the father said to his slaves, 'Quickly bring out the best robe and put it on him, and put a ring on his hand and sandals on his feet; and bring the fattened calf, kill it, and let us eat and be merry; for this son of mine was dead, and has come to life again; he was lost, and has been found.' And they began to be merry."

III. Our Dealings with an Older Rebel

If you have a rebel at home who wants to break with the family, here are some important principles to consider.

A. No rebellious child should be allowed to ruin a home. No matter how gifted, no rebel should be saved at the sacrifice of the entire family. John White adds a helpful dimension to this dilemma.

> The decision to dismiss children from home should not be made either because it will work or as a matter of expediency. It should be made on the basis of justice. And justice must consider every side of the problem. Is it morally just to keep children at

home when other family members suffer deprivation in one form or another because of them?[4]

B. Principle must prevail over the person. Again, justice must rule, impartially and without respect to persons—even if that person is your child. If an eternal principle is at stake, as with Eli's sons, stand on the principle, even if that means standing against your own flesh and blood. Take a look at some further wisdom from John White.

> God respected the dignity of our primal forefathers. He could have prevented their tragic disobedience and could thus have circumvented all the tragedies of human existence. He gave them a choice. They chose rebellion. He was then obliged to drive them from the garden.
>
> If God so respects the autonomy he gave us, then we also must do the same for our children. In their earliest years they are not ready to be given full control of their lives because they are too vulnerable, too weak, too inexperienced to use it. But when the time comes, and that time must be decided by the parents as they wait on God, we must give them the dignity of letting them face the real consequences of their actions.
>
> To do so will be painful. If ever you find yourself in that position, beware of sealing your heart in bitterness. The test of godly maturity will be to carry out the sentence combining tenderness with firmness.[5]

C. When true repentance occurs, God honors a forgiving response and a loving welcome. The parable of the prodigal son should really be titled the parable of the compassionate father. For it is not the repentance of the son that overwhelms us; it's the all-embracing love of the father. And as the parable implies, when we joyfully embrace repentant sinners, we are most like our Father in heaven. This mental picture not only brings sinners back to God, but rebellious children back to the waiting arms of their parents.

---

4. White, *Parents in Pain,* pp. 204–5. Used by permission.
5. White, *Parents in Pain,* pp. 206–7. Used by permission.

Living Insights

Study One ▬▬▬▬▬▬▬▬▬▬▬▬▬▬▬▬▬▬▬▬▬▬▬▬▬▬▬▬

Have you ever taken the time to ponder the meaning of the parable of the prodigal son? Perhaps you're so familiar with the story that it's lost its punch. Let's remedy this situation.

• Read Luke 15:11–24 in another version of the Bible. This exercise will help you gain fresh insights into this well-known account. Read slowly and thoughtfully. Ask God to show you something special.

 Living Insights

Study Two ▬▬▬▬▬▬▬▬▬▬▬▬▬▬▬▬▬▬▬▬▬▬▬▬▬▬▬▬

What should you do with an older rebel in your family? Many parents are dealing with this issue right now, others already have, and some will experience it later.

• Do you have a strategy for dealing with rebellion in your older children? You'll need to be flexible and sensitive to the individual situation, but try to think of some eternal principles that are not up for discussion . . . things that are absolute principles from God.

How I Will Deal with an Older Rebel

_____

_____

_____

_____

_____

_____

_____

_____

_____

_____

_____

_____

Equipping the Family
for the Unforeseen
Job 1–2

If we want to grow wise in family life, we have to give up some of our fantasies.

We like to view the family through the sentimental wire rims of Norman Rockwell: Father is at the head of the table, carving the Thanksgiving turkey; Mother is wearing her unsoiled apron, beaming over the meal in matronly elegance; children are gathered dutifully around the table—eager, wide-eyed, and rosy-cheeked. Truly a cornucopian Thanksgiving.

In real life, though, Dad is probably snoring on the couch to the tunes of halftime marching bands blaring from the TV. Mom is a limp dishrag after hours in the hot kitchen with a turkey that's too dry, dressing that's too soggy, gravy that's too lumpy, and rolls that are burnt on the bottom. And the kids? Well, the younger ones are pulling each other's hair out in the den; the pubescent son is locked in his room, his CD player throbbing to some *alien pulse* while he's chewing gum as if it were one of the four basic food groups. And the older daughter has been on the phone so long that, when she finally comes to the table, her head is fixed at a right angle.

Now that's real life. And taking a good look at it is the only way to get equipped for the unforeseen.

I. Life as It Is . . . Not as We Would Imagine
Cinderellas generally don't marry charming princes. Too few children can say with Dorothy, "There's no place like home." And in the real world, Father doesn't always know best. If we're going to see life as it really is, we must strip away our illusions. When you get down to basics, life consists of four key areas: people, events, decisions, and results.

A. People. Basically, by virtue of the Fall, people are sinful, selfish, and going through some kind of trouble.[1] We imagine, however, that they are good, giving, and living happily ever after.

B. Events. Many events that happen in our lives are unpredictable and surprising. We imagine, though, that to a large extent we can shape our destiny and predict what will happen.

C. Decisions. Many decisions we make are horizontal in scope and not necessarily aligned to biblical principles. We imagine,

---

1. In contrasting the deeds of the flesh with the fruit of the Spirit, Paul shows which fruit grows naturally out of our old nature and which fruit sprouts naturally from our new nature (Gal. 5:19–23). In Ephesians 4:22–32 he again describes the two natures and shows that what springs out of the old self is a Pandora's box of sinful and self-serving deeds.

though, that our orientation is vertical. We believe that we received our marching orders from God when, in fact, we may have listened to society's drumbeat instead.

D. Results. The ramifications of our decisions are often far-reaching and painful to others. But we tend to imagine that we are autonomous beings and that our decisions affect only ourselves.

II. Life as It Was . . . Not as We Would Expect

Paging through the Scriptures, our thumb stops at the oldest book in the Bible—Job. Here we find the most ideal family we could possibly imagine.

A. An enviable family. Beginning with Job himself, we see that he was an ideal father.

> There was a man in the land of Uz, whose name was
> Job, and that man was blameless, upright, fearing
> God, and turning away from evil. (1:1)

So widespread was Job's renown that he was recognized as "the greatest of all the men of the east" (v. 3b). He had a wife and ten children (v. 2). He was affluent (v. 3). His children got along well (v. 4). And, most of all, Job took his relationship with the Lord seriously (v. 5). It seems that Job's family life would have been a perfect picture for Norman Rockwell to capture on canvas. But as we will see, the colors on the palette turn suddenly dark and somber.

B. A series of calamities. Without a whisper of warning, Job's well-ordered life came crashing down around him like a house of cards. Within a span of minutes, four messengers reported to Job their devastating news.

> Now it happened on the day when his sons and his
> daughters were eating and drinking wine in their old-
> est brother's house, that a messenger came to Job
> and said, "The oxen were plowing and the donkeys
> feeding beside them, and the Sabeans attacked and
> took them. They also slew the servants with the edge
> of the sword, and I alone have escaped to tell you."
> While he was still speaking, another also came and
> said, "The fire of God fell from heaven and burned
> up the sheep and the servants and consumed them,
> and I alone have escaped to tell you." While he was
> still speaking, another also came and said, "The Chal-
> deans formed three bands and made a raid on the
> camels and took them and slew the servants with the
> edge of the sword; and I alone have escaped to tell
> you." While he was still speaking, another also came
> and said, "Your sons and your daughters were eating

and drinking wine in their oldest brother's house, and behold, a great wind came from across the wilderness and struck the four corners of the house, and it fell on the young people and they died; and I alone have escaped to tell you." (vv. 13–19)

As we see Job's suffering, we easily share in his sorrow. What's not so easy is sharing his submissive response.

Then Job arose and tore his robe and shaved his head, and he fell to the ground and worshiped. And he said,

"Naked I came from my mother's womb,
And naked I shall return there.
The Lord gave and the Lord has taken
away.
Blessed be the name of the Lord."
Through all this Job did not sin nor did he blame God. (vv. 20–22)

As if this bout hasn't been grueling enough, Satan gets another round with this battered believer and strikes a vicious body blow. From head to toe, Job is afflicted with boils (2:7–8). During this painful time, even his wife emotionally deserts him (vv. 9–10), leaving him to sift through the ashes of his spiritual confusion alone.

C. **A road to recovery.** As we see Job sorting through the rubble of unforeseen tragedy, we find him steadily making progress on the road to recovery. The road will be long and winding through forty-two chapters of rugged introspection, but in the first two chapters he struggles to take four giant steps up that road. *First,* there is the agony of humanity. There is shock, grief, pain, disbelief, and panic. The text says he "tore his robe and shaved his head" and "was sitting among the ashes" (1:20a, 2:8b). These were all outward manifestations of his inward grief. *Second,* there is the struggle with theology. His wife, who couldn't make sense of the suffering, encourages him to "curse God and die" (v. 9). Surely Job wondered how God could permit such a thing and where He was during his hurt. *Third,* there is an acceptance of reality. In 2:10 he responds to his wife: " 'Shall we indeed accept good from God and not accept adversity?' " *Fourth,* there is freedom from iniquity: "Through all this Job did not sin nor did he blame God" (1:22, 2:10b). While working through grief, the tendency is to blame others, even God. But Job suspends judgment and instead submits to suffering's yoke.

┌───┐
│ ― *Asking the Right Questions* ―――――――――――――――――――   │
│   The problem of pain raises a number of thorny questions │
│   that prick the soul. But when dealing with unforeseen suffer- │
│   ing, it's important that our questions lead ultimately to God. │
│   We should go beyond the question "Why is this happen- │
│   ing to me?" and ask, "Where does it lead?" And we should │
│   see behind the question "What sense is there to the suf- │
│   fering?" and ask ourselves, "Whom does it serve—God │
│   or the devil?" │
│   It is not the circumstance itself, but our reaction to it, │
│   that determines whether the unforeseen results in trag- │
│   edy or triumph. │
└───┘

D. A remarkable restoration. Following a painfully revealing
dialogue with God, the story comes full circle and ends on a
positive, upbeat note.

> And the Lord restored the fortunes of Job when he
> prayed for his friends, and the Lord increased all that
> Job had twofold. Then all his brothers, and all his
> sisters, and all who had known him before, came to
> him, and they ate bread with him in his house; and
> they consoled him and comforted him for all the evil
> that the Lord had brought on him.[2] And each one
> gave him one piece of money, and each a ring of gold.
> And the Lord blessed the latter days of Job more
> than his beginning, and he had 14,000 sheep, and
> 6,000 camels, and 1,000 yoke of oxen, and 1,000 female
> donkeys. And he had seven sons and three daughters.
> (42:10–13)

With God's restorative touch, the gaping wound in Job's life is
closed and finally healed.

---

2. The word translated *evil* in Hebrew may also be translated as "misery, distress, injury."
The word is used about twenty times to designate injury done to the body and about a dozen
times to describe sorrow one may experience. Its use here denotes the sum of the distressing
happenings of life. See the *Theological Wordbook of the Old Testament*, ed. R. Laird Harris,
Gleason L. Archer, Jr., and Bruce K. Waltke (Chicago, Ill.: Moody Press, 1980), vol. 2, p. 856.
This verse, which attributes Job's misery to God, poses an apparent contradiction with chapter 1, which attributes his suffering to Satan. Although God did not bring misery into Job's
life Himself, by permitting Satan to do so, God can be looked at as ultimately sharing a degree
of responsibility for what Job experienced. The difference between the responsibility of Satan
and that of God was that Satan brought misery into Job's life with the intent of getting him
to defect from God (1:9–11). God's intent, however, was to display Job as an example of
integrity and patient endurance in the midst of trials (compare 2:3 with James 5:11).

III. Life as It Will Be . . . Not as We Would Prefer

As the storms of life sweep over us, we bend and sway under their force. But shallow-rooted, slow-growing creatures that we are, we prefer sunshine to torrential rain and calm, idyllic days to windswept nights. We prefer no surprises. But in spite of our preferences, life remains untamed and unpredictable. We prefer protection from adversity—a shelter from the wind and rain. But life continues its pelting downpour. We prefer to watch the lightning and hear the thunder from a distance. But God brings the clouds near. Fortunately, though, He leads us through the storm . . . hand in hand . . . a step at a time (Ps. 23:4).

 Living Insights

Study One ▬▬▬▬▬▬▬▬▬▬▬▬▬▬▬▬▬▬▬▬▬▬▬▬▬▬▬

Just when you think you have life figured out, it throws you an unforeseen curve and you're sent reeling. There's no better illustration of this in all of Scripture than the book of Job.

- Read Job 1 and 2. Write down the words you consider to be key to the meaning of the passage. Then define these terms, either from the context or with the help of a Bible dictionary. Finally, explain why you think each term is significant.

Key word: ___ _____

Definition: _____

_____

Significance: _____

_____

Key word: _____

Definition: _____

_____

Significance: _____

_____

Continued on next page

Key word: _____

Definition: _____

_____

Significance: _____

_____

Key word: _____

Definition: _____

_____

Significance: _____

_____

Key word: _____

Definition: _____

_____

Significance: _____

_____

Key word: _____

Definition: _____

_____

Significance: _____

_____

Key word: _____

Definition: _____

_____

Significance: _____

_____

Living Insights

Through the earlier part of his excruciating ordeal, Job did not sin or blame God. This provides us with a good principle to live by: When the unforeseen occurs, your spiritual life makes the difference whether the trial will temper you or break you.

● Let's use our Living Insights for a time of prayer. If you're going through a difficult time right now, tell the Lord about it. If life is going smoothly for you, talk to the Lord about your ability to cope if a trial should come. Use this as a time to get closer to Him.

Equipping the Family
for the Unbearable
2 Samuel 18:5-19:8

Few families have experienced the unbearable circumstances the Jaeger family did.

When George Jaeger took his three sons and [their] elderly grandfather out on the Atlantic Ocean for a fishing trip, he had no premonition of the horror that he would face in a matter of hours. . . .

The boat's engine had stalled in the late afternoon. While increasing winds whipped the sea into great waves, the boat rolled helpless in the water and then began to list dangerously. When it became apparent that they were sinking, the five Jaeger men put on the life vests, tied themselves together with a rope, and slipped into the water. It was 6:30 P.M. when the sinking craft disappeared and the swimmers set out to work their way toward shore.

Six-foot waves and a strong current made the swimming almost impossible. First one boy, and then another—and another . . . swallowed too much water. Helpless, George Jaeger watched his sons and then his father die. Eight hours later, he staggered onto the shore, still pulling the rope that bound the bodies of the other four to him.

"I realized they were all dead—my three boys and my father—but I guess I didn't want to accept it, so I kept swimming all night long," he said to reporters. "My youngest boy, Clifford, was the first to go. *I had always taught our children not to fear death* because it was being with Jesus Christ. Before he died I heard him say, 'I'd rather be with Jesus than go on fighting.' "[1]

In one day, a family was torn apart forever, leaving the survivors with an unbearable loss. Their pain was intense; still, the Jaegers were equipped to handle such a tragedy because they had prepared themselves for death.

Hopefully, today's lesson will prepare you to survive the storms that life may someday bring your way.

I. The Unbearable Is Inescapable
No one eludes the unbearable. It is an inescapable thorn of a fallen world, as indicated here by Job, whose name has become synonymous with suffering.

---

1. Gordon MacDonald, *The Effective Father* (Wheaton, Ill.: Tyndale House Publishers, 1977), pp. 13-14. Used by permission.

"For man is born for trouble,
As sparks fly upward." (5:7)
Again, in 14:1, Job underscores the inevitability of human suffering.
"Man, who is born of woman,
Is short-lived and full of turmoil."
When the crush of circumstances pressures us, we instinctively cry
out to God for relief. No stranger to grief himself, David records one
such cry in Psalm 102:1–7.
Hear my prayer, O Lord!
And let my cry for help come to Thee.
Do not hide Thy face from me in the day of my distress;
Incline Thine ear to me;
In the day when I call answer me quickly.
For my days have been consumed in smoke,
And my bones have been scorched like a hearth.
My heart has been smitten like grass and has withered
away,
Indeed, I forget to eat my bread.
Because of the loudness of my groaning
My bones cling to my flesh.
I resemble a pelican of the wilderness;
I have become like an owl of the waste places.
I lie awake,
I have become like a lonely bird on a housetop.

Why the Unbearable Is Essential

In spite of our cries, in spite of our pleas to know the *why*
of our pain, God is sometimes silent. Often we interpret this
silence as indifference and call into question His love. However,
reconciling human suffering with God's love is only a problem
if we attach a trivial meaning to the word *love*. C. S. Lewis
illustrates this with a poignant analogy.

Over a sketch made idly to amuse a child, an artist
may not take much trouble: he may be content to
let it go even though it is not exactly as he meant
it to be. But over the great picture of his life—
the work which he loves ... he will take endless
trouble—and would, doubtless, thereby *give* endless trouble to the picture if it were sentient. One
can imagine a sentient picture, after being rubbed
and scraped and re-commenced for the tenth time,
wishing that it were only a thumb-nail sketch whose
making was over in a minute. In the same way, it is
natural for us to wish that God had designed for us

135

> a less glorious and less arduous destiny; but then
> we are wishing not for more love but for less.[2]

II. The Unbearable Seems Unendurable

We often think the Old Testament saints had porcelain lives with smooth, polished features. But we fail to realize that, like porcelain, they all underwent the heat of some unbearable kiln. Take David, for example.

A. Family background. David sweated through much of Absalom's life, for this rebellious son brought heated turmoil to the palace (2 Sam. 13–18). Early on, Absalom became disillusioned by his father's passive response to his sister Tamar's rape. He later grew deceitful and finally disloyal to his father, leading a revolt against the throne. Absalom's actions left many people confused, a few resentful, and one enraged—Joab, David's military commander.

B. Absalom's death. During Absalom's coup, David fled from the throne rather than kill his own flesh and blood. Although their armies would soon clash in a fateful forest of oaks, the king made every effort to spare his wayward son.

> And the king charged Joab and Abishai and Ittai, saying, "Deal gently for my sake with the young man Absalom." And all the people heard when the king charged all the commanders concerning Absalom. (18:5)

The battle between Absalom's men and David's raged in the forest of Ephraim. But Absalom's forces were no match for the angry swords of David's mighty men (vv. 6–7). Absalom fled through the forest in defeat, and as he did, his long, flowing hair became entangled in the branches of a large oak tree. Like a fly caught in a web, he could not extricate himself. And with the nimble promptness of a spider, Joab rushed to devour his prey.

> Then Joab . . . took three spears in his hand and thrust them through the heart of Absalom while he was yet alive in the midst of the oak. And ten young men who carried Joab's armor gathered around and struck Absalom and killed him. (vv. 14–15)

C. David's grief. Having taken refuge at the city of Mahanaim, David was anxiously awaiting news of his son's welfare. *Is it well with Absalom? . . . Is it well with Absalom?* he begged of Joab's

---

2. C. S. Lewis, *The Problem of Pain* (New York, N.Y.: The Macmillan Co., 1962), pp. 42–43.

messengers as they arrived (vv. 29, 32). When the truth of Absalom's death finally came out, David's grief was unbearable. And the king was deeply moved[3] and went up to the chamber over the gate and wept. And thus he said as he walked, "O my son Absalom, my son, my son Absalom! Would I had died instead of you, O Absalom, my son, my son!" Then it was told Joab, "Behold, the king is weeping and mourns for Absalom." And the victory that day was turned to mourning for all the people, for the people heard it said that day, "The king is grieved for his son." So the people went by stealth into the city that day, as people who are humiliated steal away when they flee in battle. And the king covered his face and cried out with a loud voice, "O my son Absalom, O Absalom, my son, my son!" (18:33–19:4)

In *A Grief Observed,* C. S. Lewis wrote of his wife's death: "Her absence is like the sky, spread over everything."[4] This emptiness permeated David's life too, down to the depths of his soul. Not only did his son's death seem unendurable, but his grief and remorse seemed unending.

III. The Unbearable Is Not Unending

Although some pain seems unrelenting, it isn't. As Solomon said: "There is an appointed time for everything. . . . A time to weep, and a time to laugh;/A time to mourn, and a time to dance" (Eccles. 3:1a, 4). It may feel as if unbearable circumstances have wintered in your heart, but remember that seasons do change. And spring may be just around the corner. In David's life, however, winter had just fallen with an untimely frost at the news of Absalom's death.

A. Joab's counsel. Joab, who had seen the whole tragic story of Absalom's life unfolded shamefully before all Israel, confronted David about the inequity of his narrowly focused grief. In bold, blunt words, he told David to face the truth and realize how his actions were affecting those around him.

Then Joab came into the house to the king and said, "Today you have covered with shame the faces of all your servants, who today have saved your life and the lives of your sons and daughters, the lives of your

---

3. The Hebrew word is *ragaz.* "The primary meaning of this root is to quake or shake. . . . Most usages of *ragaz* express agitation growing out of some deeply rooted emotion" like trembling in fear or raging in anger. *Theological Wordbook of the Old Testament,* ed. R. Laird Harris, Gleason L. Archer, Jr., Bruce K. Waltke (Chicago, Ill.: Moody Press, 1980), vol. 2, pp. 830–31.

4. C. S. Lewis, *A Grief Observed* (New York, N.Y.: Bantam Books, 1961), p. 11.

wives, and the lives of your concubines, by loving
those who hate you, and by hating those who love
you." (19:5–6a)

David no doubt felt tremendous guilt about his relationship with
Absalom. As a result, his tears blurred the fact that Absalom had
been bent on destroying him and any of his people that stood
in the way. Enraged that David didn't see how his intense grief
was demeaning the loyalty of his people, Joab lashed out.

"For you have shown today that princes and servants
are nothing to you; for I know this day that if Absalom
were alive and all of us were dead today, then you
would be pleased." (v. 6b)

When David turned his guilt inward, it set his conscience aflame
and demoralized him. He was ashamed of his failure as a father,
knowing that it ultimately led to Absalom's destruction. So great
was his sorrow and so preoccupied was he with it, that he lost
sight of the people around him. Joab saw this and instructed
David to affirm the ones closest to him.

"Now therefore arise, go out and speak kindly to your
servants, for I swear by the Lord, if you do not go
out, surely not a man will pass the night with you,
and this will be worse for you than all the evil that
has come upon you from your youth until now." (v. 7)

Unbearable circumstances threw David into a vertigo of introspection. But Joab grabbed him by the shoulders, stood him on
the ground, and got David to take his eyes off himself and place
them onto those who were in desperate need of his affirmation.

B. David's response. The king heeded Joab's advice.

So the king arose and sat in the gate. When they told
all the people, saying, "Behold, the king is sitting
in the gate," then all the people came before the
king. (v. 8a)

The sharp edges of David's unbearable pain appear to have been
blunted once he began to mingle among the people and return
to his responsibilities of ruling the kingdom.

A Time to Weep

C. S. Lewis went through a long grieving process when
he lost his wife to cancer. You can follow the winding road
that his grief took in his book *A Grief Observed.*

In his pain, he asked searching questions about his faith.

Meanwhile, where is God?... Go to Him when
your need is desperate, when all other help is
vain, and what do you find? A door slammed in

138

> your face, and a sound of bolting and double
> bolting on the inside. After that, silence.[5]
> It's completely natural when we're shouldering unbear-
> able circumstances to cry out to God for relief. And when
> relief isn't immediate, it's easy to come to the same con-
> clusion Lewis did. As we look at Lewis's grief sometime
> later, we see that the pain was not unending.
>
> > Turned to God, my mind no longer meets that
> > locked door.... There was no sudden, striking,
> > and emotional transition. Like the warming of
> > a room or the coming of daylight. When you
> > first notice them they have already been going
> > on for some time.[6]
>
> Time does have its way of healing our wounds, and
> just as certain as there will be a time to weep, there will
> also—someday—be a time to laugh again.

IV. The Unbearable Can Be Endured

In closing, we want to distill the bubbling turmoil of David's life into
principles that can equip us to endure the unbearable. First, we need
to be realistic. Tragedy will likely touch all of us at some time or
another. But as long as we deny that reality, we won't be prepared
to handle it when it does come. Second, we need a friend who is
honest. David's life was filled with such friends, tracing back to
Jonathan and Nathan. We all need friends who can put an arm
around us while telling us the truth . . . friends like the one described
in Proverbs 27:5–6.

> Better is open rebuke
> Than love that is concealed.
> Faithful are the wounds of a friend,
> But deceitful are the kisses of an enemy.

And although Joab wasn't the perfect model of a friend, he was
forthright to David about his feelings. Third, we need a Savior who
is reliable, who is the same yesterday, today, and forever (Heb. 13:8);
who will never leave or forsake us no matter what happens (v. 5);
and who will be with us always, taking our hand as we go up the
hills or down through the valleys (Matt. 28:20b). We have such a
Savior in the Lord Jesus, who's waiting for us to turn to Him in our
unbearable situations. Finally, we need a faith that is sure, a faith
that realizes all of our experiences are not intrinsically good, but in
God's redemptive grace they work together *for* good (Rom. 8:28).

5. Lewis, *A Grief Observed,* p. 4.
6. Lewis, *A Grief Observed,* p. 71.

Living Insights

What a comfort it is to find someone who has experienced the same pain you have, who understands what you're feeling. The pages of Scripture reveal many people who lived through unbearable situations. Their stories are preserved so we can both learn and gain comfort from them.

• Throughout the ages, the Word of God has been an anchor for those in agony. Which Scripture verses do you turn to when going through difficult times? Take this opportunity to memorize some of those passages so you'll have them ready when you need them. If you've already memorized them, meditate on them or memorize some new ones.

 Living Insights

How can we endure the unbearable? In this lesson we learned four principles that will help us. In the space provided, evaluate how these needs are being met in your life.

• I need to be realistic.

• I need a friend who is honest.

• I need a Savior who is reliable.

• I need a faith that is sure.

Equipping the Family for the Unusual

Genesis 6–9, Hebrews 11:7

Charlie Steinmetz had one of the greatest minds in electronics that the world has ever known. In fact, he built the mammoth generators for Henry Ford's first automobile plant in Dearborn, Michigan. One day, one of those generators broke down, and the plant screeched to a halt. Unable to get the generator going again, Ford called Steinmetz.

He came and puttered around the plant for a few hours. Tinkering with a few gauges, Steinmetz turned this, adjusted that, and then threw a switch that put the massive plant back into operation.

A few days later, Ford received a bill from Steinmetz for $10,000. Surprised, Ford returned the bill with this note: "Charlie, isn't this bill just a little high for a few hours of tinkering around on those motors?"

Steinmetz returned an itemized bill to Ford:

For Tinkering Around on the Motors:	$ 10
For Knowing *Where* to Tinker:	9,990
Total:	$10,000

Ford paid the bill with a smile. For what appeared to be of little value was, in fact, of greatest value—an entire assembly line depended on Steinmetz's knowledge.[1]

We've been tinkering with the subject of how to equip families for life. But behind the scenes, tapping gauges and turning switches, is the Holy Spirit. And He knows just where to tinker, doesn't He?

We've puttered around with the subject of the unforeseen and the unbearable. Now we want to turn our attention to the unusual so we can be equipped to understand God's standard operating procedure.

I. In God's Family . . . An Unusual Operating Procedure

God's *modus operandi* is the great, the unsearchable, and the miraculous, as Eliphaz confirms in Job 5.

"But as for me, I would seek God,
And I would place my cause before God;
Who does great and unsearchable things,
Wonders without number." (vv. 8–9)

In verses 10–16, we see the uncommon and unusual ways God works in people's lives.

---

1. David A. Seamands, *Healing for Damaged Emotions* (Wheaton, Ill.: Victor Books, 1981), p. 23.

"He gives rain on the earth,
And sends water on the fields,
So that He sets on high those who are lowly,
And those who mourn are lifted to safety.
He frustrates the plotting of the shrewd,
So that their hands cannot attain success.
He captures the wise by their own shrewdness
And the advice of the cunning is quickly thwarted.
By day they meet with darkness,
And grope at noon as in the night.
But He saves from the sword of their mouth,
And the poor from the hand of the mighty.
So the helpless has hope,
And unrighteousness must shut its mouth."

God's incredible workings give hope to the lowly and meager, while dumbfounding the high and mighty. The New Testament counterpart to this passage is Romans 11:33.

Oh, the depth of the riches both of the wisdom and knowledge of God! How unsearchable are His judgments and unfathomable His ways!

Stop for a minute and think through the Bible. It's just bursting at the seams with the incredible ways God works. The parting of the Red Sea. Manna from heaven. The pillars of cloud and fire to guide Israel in the wilderness. Jericho's wall. The virgin birth. Water into wine. Feeding the five thousand. Healing after healing. The Resurrection. And the list goes on and on. God still desires to do the unusual and the unsearchable . . . but are we open to that? Are we ready? Are we willing to let Him work in unusual ways?

II. In Noah's Family . . . A Study in Surprises

Noah's family was no different than ours—with one exception. They were open, ready, and willing to be a part of God's plan, even if that plan seemed highly unusual.

A. Difficult times in which to live. Noah and his family grew up in an ungodly culture. Depravity paraded the streets in a raucous Mardi Gras of immorality.

Then the Lord saw that the wickedness of man was great on the earth, and that every intent of the thoughts of his heart was only evil continually. And the Lord was sorry that He had made man on the earth, and He was grieved in His heart. . . . Now the earth was corrupt in the sight of God, and the earth was filled with violence. And God looked on the earth, and behold, it was corrupt; for all flesh had corrupted their way upon the earth. (Gen. 6:5–6, 11–12)

Lest we place too much emphasis on the environment's role in shaping character, note that in the midst of this cesspool society there arose an unsoiled saint.

But Noah found favor in the eyes of the Lord. These are the records of the generations of Noah. Noah was a righteous man, blameless in his time; Noah walked with God. (vv. 8–9)

Righteous before God and blameless before others, Noah was like a salmon swimming upstream against the swift and sordid currents of his culture.

B. **A frightening prophecy and a creative plan.** In verses 7, 13, and 17 God unveiled a sobering glimpse of the brimming caldron of His wrath.

And the Lord said, "I will blot out man whom I have created from the face of the land, from man to animals to creeping things and to birds of the sky; for I am sorry that I have made them." . . . Then God said to Noah, "The end of all flesh has come before Me; for the earth is filled with violence because of them; and behold, I am about to destroy them with the earth. . . . And behold, I, even I am bringing the flood of water upon the earth, to destroy all flesh in which is the breath of life, from under heaven; everything that is on the earth shall perish."

But before God's wrath spilled over to inundate the world, God arranged a creative plan of deliverance.

"Make for yourself an ark of gopher wood; you shall make the ark with rooms, and shall cover it inside and out with pitch. And this is how you shall make it: the length of the ark three hundred cubits, its breadth fifty cubits, and its height thirty cubits." (vv. 14–15)

This ark would measure 450 feet long, 75 feet wide, and 45 feet high[2] and have the same volume as 522 livestock railroad cars.[3] This request was highly unusual because *it had never rained before,* let alone flooded (2:5–6). But while a reprobate world scorned, God was in the process of saving a remnant—a small scrap of humanity who still believed in Him, still loved Him, still served Him (6:18–21).

2. These figures are based on a cubit of eighteen inches.

3. Henry M. Morris, *The Genesis Record* (Grand Rapids, Mich.: Baker Book House, 1976), p. 181.

C. Obedience, deliverance, and a blessing. Noah obeyed God and built the ark (v. 22), a task that took his family 120 years to complete (v. 3). At last the day came that would seal the fate of a decadent world.

> Then the Lord said to Noah, "Enter the ark, you and all your household; for you alone I have seen to be righteous before Me in this time." (7:1)

Again Noah's obedience is underscored: "And Noah did according to all that the Lord had commanded" (v. 5). For forty days and forty nights the rains came (v. 12). Yet in the midst of this destruction, God's deliverance was at work, saving everyone and everything in the ark (v. 23). When the water dried up, Noah built an altar to thank Him for taking them safely through the storm (8:20–21). And God responded with His blessing.

> And God blessed Noah and his sons and said to them, "Be fruitful and multiply, and fill the earth." (9:1)

D. A rainbow and a reminder. To remind Noah of His covenant with the earth, God established a beautiful visual aid for all generations.

> And God said, "This is the sign of the covenant which I am making between Me and you and every living creature that is with you, for all successive generations; I set My bow in the cloud, and it shall be for a sign of a covenant between Me and the earth. And it shall come about, when I bring a cloud over the earth, that the bow shall be seen in the cloud, and I will remember My covenant, which is between Me and you and every living creature of all flesh; and never again shall the water become a flood to destroy all flesh. When the bow is in the cloud, then I will look upon it, to remember the everlasting covenant between God and every living creature of all flesh that is on the earth." And God said to Noah, "This is the sign of the covenant which I have established between Me and all flesh that is on the earth." (vv. 12–17)

As a hunter might have bronzed his bow and arrows and displayed them on a fireplace mantle to indicate the end of his hunting days, so God blazoned His bow in the sky. Never again would He use rain to pour out His wrath upon the earth.

> *Living by Faith*
> Because of his incredible trust in God, Noah has been enshrined in the Hall of Faith of Hebrews 11.

144

> By faith Noah, being warned by God about things
> not yet seen, in reverence prepared an ark for
> the salvation of his household, by which he con-
> demned the world, and became an heir of the
> righteousness which is according to faith. (v. 7)
> God asked Noah to believe some pretty incredible things
> —like the coming of a worldwide flood when he had never
> even seen rain. God also asked Noah to do some incredible
> things—like taking 120 years out of his life to build a boat.
> Yet he trusted. And he obeyed.
> By faith, Noah believed God's warning. By faith, he
> obeyed by building the ark. And by faith, he became an
> heir of righteousness.
> Is God asking you to believe and do some pretty in-
> credible things right now? To trust Him when those around
> you are calling you a fool for doing so? Remember, they
> called Noah a fool too. And while he was on his way to
> Hebrews 11, they were left behind—treading water.

III. In Your Family . . . Some Practical Suggestions

Noah and his family model the importance of following God, even
if the path of obedience is highly unusual, even if the road is steep,
the way rocky, and the visibility poor. Here are a few suggestions
that will better equip your family for the unusual. First, remind your
family that the unusual is God's standard operating procedure.
Second, keep in mind that He is still looking for families who will
model His message. He is eager to write additional verses for
Hebrews 11, and maybe one of those verses has your family's name
on it. Third, fight the tendency to prefer security over availability,
to prefer today's comfort over tomorrow's challenge. Finally, listen
to your children when they urge you to do the unusual. Remember,
God often speaks through them too. After all, the children were the
ones who recognized Jesus as the Messiah and sang His praise, while
the adults criticized from afar (Matt. 21:15–16).

 Living Insights

Study One ▬▬▬▬▬▬▬▬▬▬▬▬▬▬▬▬▬▬▬▬▬▬▬

In her excellent book *Walking on Water,* Madeleine L'Engle privileges
us with a peek into her journal, showing us the road her faith has taken.
One of the quotes that was especially dear to her in defining a life of
faith was from Emmanuel, Cardinal Suhard:

"To be a witness does not consist in engaging in propaganda, nor even in stirring people up, but in being a living mystery. It means to live in such a way that one's life would not make sense if God did not exist."[4]

A living mystery. That was Noah all right, living his life in such a way that it could only make sense if God existed. How about your life? Are you a living mystery? Or have you played it safe, hedging your bets to make sure you won't look like a fool? Do people look at your life, as they did Noah's, and scratch their heads, wondering what in the world you're up to now? If not, maybe you're not building a big enough boat. Maybe you're not trusting God for the unusual.

- Write a list of a few unusual things that God may be asking you to trust Him about—things on scale with Noah's ark.

_____

_____

_____

_____

_____

Remind yourself that the unusual is God's standard operating procedure, and spend a few minutes praying about those things you wrote down. Pray that you would be available—available to do what God wants you to do or to go where He wants you to go. Who knows where that kind of faith might take you? Maybe to the hallowed halls of Hebrews 11!

 Living Insights

Study Two ▬▬▬▬▬▬▬▬▬▬▬▬▬▬▬▬▬▬▬▬▬▬

Part of the battle plan for handling the unforeseen, the unbearable, and the unusual involves communicating our difficulties with someone who cares. The help of a friend is more than a luxury; it's a necessity.

- Plan a time to sit down with a good friend to discuss the recent events of your life. Share both the victories and the defeats. Fine tune your accountability to this person. You'll benefit greatly from this person's listening ear and supportive words.

---

4. Madeleine L'Engle, *Walking on Water: Reflections on Faith and Art* (Wheaton, Ill.: Harold Shaw Publishers, 1980), p. 31.

What to Do
When You've Blown It
Selected Scripture

If only.

Two words with slumped shoulders and downcast eyes that so often follow us through life. "If only I had known. . . . If only I could take back what I said. . . . If only I could undo what I did. . . ."

If only.

Words of regret. Words of shamed remembrance. Words that admit we've blown it.

The discouraging thing about studying Scripture is that we see how many mistakes we've made in life. Intellectual mistakes. Spiritual mistakes. Conversational mistakes. The list goes on and on.

But no mistakes are as painful as people mistakes. Especially mistakes made with people we love—like our children.

Although it's impossible to turn back the clock, we *can* turn the negative memories of those mistakes into something positive.

I. Inescapable and Painful Realities of Humanity

"To err is human" is a shopworn sign we could all hang over our lives. No matter how much we regret them, mistakes are an inescapable part of our humanity. We are all imperfect—including our offspring. We cannot change the past—including the way we raised our children. And we are personally responsible for our own mistakes—including even innocent ones. A hastily woven blanket of rationalization can cover our mistakes with flimsy excuses, but it doesn't make them disappear. And an accusing finger pointed at others doesn't diffuse the blame; it only confuses it.

II. Guidelines for Recovery and Renewal

So how do we recover from the mistakes we've already made? For an alcoholic, the first step of recovery is to look people in the eye and say: "Hello. My name is so and so. I'm an alcoholic." This honesty and forthrightness is also needed by parents when they take that first step on the road to recovery after blowing it. Several guidelines will help you choose the right path to renewed relationships with your children.

A. Negatively: things that *won't* help. Admitting your mistakes is an important step to overcoming them. But it won't help to think: "It's all my fault." Problems in relationships are seldom

147

just one person's responsibility, even in parent-child relationships. Parenting, at its best, is a complex and demanding task. At its worst, it's a no-win situation that can produce the most frustrating guilt trip in all of life. Although we are imperfect parents, we are not the antecedent to all our children's problems— even God, the only perfect parent, has trouble with His less-than-perfect children. John White underscores this in his excellent book *Parents in Pain:*

> Parents are admonished to bring up children properly. Children are admonished to respond wisely to parental correction. If both play their part all will be well. But it takes a parent-child team working in harmony to produce this happy result.[1]

Later in his book White comments:

> You cannot ever control another human being, even if that human being is your own child.[2]

Another thing to avoid is being too simplistic in our use of Scripture verses and biblical principles. God's Word is the light that guides our way, but it is not Aladdin's lamp. We can't rub it three times and—abracadabra!—expect a genie to appear and grant us our wishes. Proverbs 22:6 is a good case in point.

> Train up a child in the way he should go,
> Even when he is old he will not depart from it.

This verse usually holds true. But it is given to us as a principle, not as an absolute promise. As we all know, no matter how well taught they were in their youth, some children become prodigals. A good way to keep from making absolutes out of general principles is to avoid shackling them to words like *never* and *always*. Another way is to distinguish biblical principles from promises. Promises are *invariably* so; principles are *usually* so.

B. Positively: things that *will* help. In principle, there is a correlation in Isaiah 58 between how a nation can recover and how a parent can. Although Isaiah wrote thousands of years ago to the Jewish nation, as we dust off his words we find they are as applicable today as they were the day they were written. The context of the passage finds Israel in ruin. God counsels the people not to go through the motions of fasting and repentance. Rather, He recommends a different kind of fasting.

> "Is this not the fast which I choose,
> To loosen the bonds of wickedness,

1. John White, *Parents in Pain* (Downers Grove, Ill.: InterVarsity Press, 1979), p. 44. Used by permission.
2. White, *Parents in Pain,* p. 58. Used by permission.

To undo the bands of the yoke,
And to let the oppressed go free,
And break every yoke?" (v. 6)

What God was looking for was a broken and contrite heart. This would provide the bedrock upon which He would rebuild their lives and their nation. Verses 7–12 show us five important truths that laid a sturdy foundation for Israel's recovery and renewal.

1. **Humble yourself.** God wanted to see a humility of heart, one that would lower itself to extend a hand to the hungry and the homeless.

> "Is it not to divide your bread with the hungry,
> And bring the homeless poor into the house;
> When you see the naked, to cover him;
> And not to hide yourself from your own flesh?
> Then your light will break out like the dawn,
> And your recovery will speedily spring forth;
> And your righteousness will go before you;
> The glory of the Lord will be your rear guard."
> (vv. 7–8)

The biggest obstacle to humility is pride. Pride keeps our necks stiff and our backs straight, a posture that has trouble bending to reach out to others. By way of application, if we lower ourselves in humility and admit our failure to our children, we will have taken a giant step toward recovery. As you relate to your children, is your attitude so fixed and rigid that you can't get down on their level?

2. **Pray.** A natural result of a humble heart is prayer.

> "Then you will call, and the Lord will answer;
> You will cry, and He will say, 'Here I am.'"
> (v. 9a)

Just as it was necessary for the Israelites to pray for their nation, so it is necessary for us to pray for our children as we try to rebuild the broken walls in our relationships. When was the last time you prayed for yours?

3. **Remove the yoke.** The next bit of rubble the nation had to clear away is found in the second half of verse 9.

> "Remove the yoke from your midst,
> The pointing of the finger, and speaking wicked-
> ness."

Do you want to break the constricting yoke that chafes your relationship with your children? Then ease the heavy load of blame from their shoulders—relax the pointing finger and soften the accusing voice . . . and lighten up a little.

4. Make yourself available and vulnerable. Verses 10–11 tell us that the way to satisfy yourself is to give yourself for the needs of others.

"And if you give yourself to the hungry,
And satisfy the desire of the afflicted,
Then your light will rise in darkness,
And your gloom will become like midday.
And the Lord will continually guide you,
And satisfy your desire in scorched places,
And give strength to your bones;
And you will be like a watered garden,
And like a spring of water whose waters do not
    fail."

Are you available to your children when they hunger for attention? Are you supportive when their esteem is afflicted? There is great encouragement here to all of us who've blown it. No matter how dark the shadows that stalk us from the past, God can dispel those haunting memories with the light of His grace.

5. Trust God to bring the changes. The nation was in a ramshackle condition, but it could be rebuilt. It would have to be done from the ground up, but God would give His people the strength to do it.

"And those from among you will rebuild the
    ancient ruins;
You will raise up the age-old foundations;
And you will be called the repairer of the breach,
The restorer of the streets in which to dwell."
(v. 12)

Can the rubble of a ruined relationship with a child take any less work? When your children see you investing your time in rebuilding the ruins, things have a good chance of changing, especially your children's perspective of you. They will begin to see you as a repairer and a restorer instead of a destroyer. In His time and in His way, God can rebuild relationships and restore foundations that were torn down years ago.

III. Essentials along the Way When Seeking to Rebuild

As you go to your child seeking to rebuild your relationship, here are three essential things to keep in mind. Think of these essentials as your mortar and trowel. First, *have the right motive*. Be honest— don't manipulate your child. Second, *be patient*. It took time for your relationship with your child to get where it is today. It's only reasonable that the rebuilding process could take as long—and take much more work. Third, *do it all in God's strength.* Invariably, God's strength manifests itself in our weakness (2 Cor. 12:9–10, Phil. 4:13). When a dog finally realizes it cannot win a fight, it shows its submission and surrenders by lying down at the stronger dog's feet, baring its throat and belly to its opponent. It's an extremely vulnerable position, but that's how the dog's life is spared. Won't you give up the fight and be vulnerable with your child? That's how God's strength will triumph. And that's when He will begin restoring the relationship.

 Living Insights

Study One ▬▬▬▬▬▬▬▬▬▬▬▬▬▬▬▬▬▬▬▬

Parents who have blown it often take all the blame and live in endless guilt. But if we stop and think for a minute, we'll remember that the Bible is full of encouragement for those who make mistakes. God is there, waiting to help.

● Use your Bible concordance to begin a list of Scriptures dealing with blowing it. You might want to start by looking up *confession, guilt, forgiveness, failure,* and *grace.* Next to each Scripture reference jot down a summary of the passage.

The Bible and Blowing It	
Scripture	Summary

Continued on next page

Scripture	Summary

 Living Insights

Study Two ▬▬▬▬▬▬▬▬▬▬▬▬▬▬▬▬▬▬▬▬▬▬▬▬▬▬▬▬▬▬▬

It is axiomatic: Confession is good for the soul. Opening the lines of communication is a vital part of recovering from past mistakes.

• Take this time to write a letter . . . to your parent, child, or both. Write about things you've learned, mistakes you've made, successes you've achieved, rebuilding you'd like to begin. Pray first; then write from your heart.

Looking Back on Things That Matter

Selected Scripture

Beyond being a book of words, the dictionary is a chronicle of our times. Its entries come and go with the tide of usage—old words disappear or gain the label "archaic"; new words find their place as technology, politics, and teenagers besiege us with their ever-evolving terms. And definitions are appended as familiar words take on new meanings.

Some say it takes as long as fifteen years for a new word or definition to find its way into Webster's—if that's true, we should soon be seeing a new entry following the word *family*. The definition most of us have grown up with has become obsolete.

> ¹**fam·i·ly** \ 'fam-(e-)lē \ *n, pl* **-lies**...**5:** the basic unit in society having as its nucleus two or more adults living together and cooperating in the care and rearing of their own or adopted children.¹

It's time to take a look at the family as it is today, with all its bumps and bruises and scars. It's time to realize how far we've wandered and to begin looking for the way home.

I. A Few Words of Clarification

A generation ago, dishwashers and clothes dryers were new inventions. Television was black and white, and VCRs weren't even dreamed of. Since then, reel-to-reel tapes have given way to eight-tracks, then to cassettes, and now to compact discs . . . and the family has given way to society's moral innovations.

A. In a cultural malaise. It wasn't long ago that a divorce was scandalous news; today, wedding rings are exchanged as temporarily as ID bracelets. It used to be that a mother and father raised their children together; today, it's as common for a child to be raised by only one natural parent as it is by both. Until recently, the home was a place of stability and security; today, it is too often filled with violence and conflict, with distrust, neglect, and open abuse. So turbulent are most homes in our country that one study has declared the American home the most dangerous place to be, outside of war.

B. From a biblical perspective. The modern family has strayed a long way from the traditional definition, but it has wandered even farther from the model found in Scripture. Like the animals, man was created male and female. But unlike the animals, man

---

1. *Webster's Ninth New Collegiate Dictionary,* see "family."

153

was created in the image of God, able to reason and choose. So along with our masculinity and femininity, God gave us marriage. And He even went one step further. Far from throwing us in the deep end of a relationship to sink or swim, He gave us the basic guidelines for a good marriage. And they're recorded for us in Genesis 2:24–25.

> For this cause a man shall *leave* his father and his mother, and shall *cleave* to his wife; and they shall *become one flesh.* And the man and his wife were *both naked and were not ashamed.* (emphasis added)

Four one-word principles: Severance. Permanence. Unity. Intimacy. God's perfect plan for an important relationship, followed up throughout Scripture with instructions for relating to one another and raising children (see Deut. 6, 11:18–21; Prov. 22:6, 15 and 29:15, 17; Eph. 5:22–6:4; 1 Pet. 3:1–7).

That Was Then . . . This Is Now

God's guidelines for families are relevant for all times and cultures, yet society changes the rules as often as it changes decades. J. Allan Petersen, in his book *The Myth of the Greener Grass,* comments on the shift in views of marital fidelity.

> A call for fidelity in the '80s is like a solitary voice crying in today's sexual wilderness. What was once labeled adultery and carried a stigma of guilt and embarrassment now is an affair—a nice-sounding, almost inviting word wrapped in mystery, fascination, and excitement. A relationship, not sin. What was once behind the scenes—a secret closely guarded—is now in the headlines, a TV theme, a best seller, as common as the cold. Marriages are "open"; divorces are "creative."[2]

II. In Light of This . . . What Really Matters?

Family life is crowded with things that seem crucial—potty training, settling sibling rivalry, budgeting, setting rules for dating, household chores—the list is endless. But when it comes right down to it, what in life *really* matters? The Bible offers us some threads of wisdom to weave into the fabric of our homes.

---

2. J. Allan Petersen, *The Myth of the Greener Grass* (Wheaton, Ill.: Tyndale House Publishers, 1983), pp. 13–14.

A. Biblical principles are more important than traditional opinions. In Matthew 15:1-6 the Pharisees are nitpicking Jesus about religious customs—His disciples are not following the Jewish tradition of washing their hands before they eat. Jesus, cutting a clear line between folk wisdom and Scripture, replies:

> "And why do you yourselves transgress the commandment of God for the sake of your tradition? For God said, 'Honor your father and mother,' and, 'He who speaks evil of father or mother, let him be put to death.' But you say, 'Whoever shall say to his father or mother, "Anything of mine you might have been helped by has been given to God," he is not to honor his father or his mother.' And thus you invalidated the word of God for the sake of your tradition." (vv. 3–6)

Folk wisdom is ingrained in our society too. How many times have you heard things like "Don't sweat the small stuff"... "What's good for one is good for all"... "Sibling rivalry will work itself out"... "The teenage years are always miserable"? So often we take those words to heart, yet their meaning is contradicted by Scripture. Of course, not all adages are unsound. To some, in fact, God probably gives a hearty nod. But they all need to be weighed against Scripture. Are you listening to your neighbor when you should be looking to God's Word?

B. Personal relationships are more valuable than individual accomplishments. In Mark 6:6b-13 we see Jesus sending his disciples out to teach and preach God's message in the face of strong opposition. When they return, Jesus recognizes their need to be together and rest.

> And He said to them, "Come away by yourselves to a lonely place and rest a while." (v. 31a)

Ours is a greedy, grabbing world. Hard-driving. High-achieving. One extra day at the office, one more parent working, a few more irons in the church or community fire. Whether by our desires, our egos, or simply other people's needs, we are pulled in a dozen different directions at once. And the people who need us most rarely see us.

Count the Cost

The decisions we make today have far-reaching effects on our family's lives. Yet we so often make those decisions with little thought.

155

> Before committing yourself to a project or accepting a new promotion, do you think about the long-term sacrifices your family will have to live with? Do your choices reflect what's most important to you? Do you find yourself choosing rewards over relationships?
>
> Take the time to ask yourself what that new car, that bigger house, that corner office is *really* costing you. Are you sure you—and your family—can afford it?

C. Domestic priorities rate higher than church programs. First Timothy 3 gives us a list of qualifications for a church official, and verses 4–5 are aimed directly at the official who's a family man.

> He must be one who manages his own household well, keeping his children under control with all dignity (but if a man does not know how to manage his own household, how will he take care of the church of God?).

Whether we are church leaders or churchgoers, the priority is the same—home comes first. Some churches are reluctant to embrace this principle. They have so intermingled commitment to church with commitment to Christ that they see them as one and the same, and their demands on our time reflect it. But sometimes the problem lies within us. We prefer being at church to being at home. It's easier. We can take notes and join groups, and no one knows how little or how much we apply. Being home demands greater honesty, deeper intimacy, and we're exposed for who we are underneath the pious tie and three-piece suit.

D. Positive acceptance is better reinforcement than negative reactions. Ephesians 6:1–4 lays out a pattern every family member should pin to their hearts.

> Children, obey your parents in the Lord, for this is right. Honor your father and mother (which is the first commandment with a promise), that it may be well with you, and that you may live long on the earth. And, fathers, do not provoke your children to anger; but bring them up in the discipline and instruction of the Lord.

How much dissension in families can be traced to the disobedience of these two simple commands! It's natural for parents to focus on the first part of that passage. But how much easier it is for children to honor parents who stop short of exasperating them. It's tough to keep responding well to someone who fills your ears with "no" and "not tonight" and "maybe some other time." Keep an open mind to your children's requests. Balance the instructions with invitations. If you're open to saying *yes* every time it's reasonable, your *no*s will be a lot easier to accept.

E. Unconditional forgiveness is better than lingering probation. Ephesians 4:32 designs the atmosphere of a happy home.

> And be kind to one another, tender-hearted, forgiving each other, just as God in Christ also has forgiven you.

Children misbehave—sometimes by mistake, and sometimes with a mischievous gleam in their eyes. And even through their protests, they long to be disciplined. But they also long for forgiveness and acceptance. Let kindness permeate your home.

The Father Who Didn't Forgive

In many ways, David is the hero of our hearts. He's our discipler in devotion, our sweet-voiced singer of psalms. But David, like all people and all parents, made mistakes he lived to regret. One was forgiveness he was too late in giving (see 2 Sam. 14:1–19:4).

David neglected his family. In the absence of a strong and involved father, one son raped David's daughter, and another son, Absalom, had the rapist killed. Absalom, in his grief and fear, fled to live with his maternal grandfather, the one person he felt secure with. And when David was finally convinced to let his son come home, he refused to see him. For two years they lived that way—in close proximity, but with no contact. And finally, Absalom led an insurrection against his father, the man who had deprived his children of a father's protection, love, and acceptance. In that insurrection Absalom was killed, and at last the enormity of David's mistake overwhelmed him.

> And the king covered his face and cried out with a loud voice, "O my son Absalom, O Absalom, my son, my son!" (19:4)

Finally, David's heart melted in forgiveness toward his son . . . but there was no longer a son to forgive.

How long will you wait to forgive and forget your child's mistakes? Don't put it off, please, because there may come a time when it will be too late.

F. Mutual respect is of greater importance than chain of command. Children don't respect parents who preach at them; they respect parents who model the truth they talk about.

And they respect parents who respect them. If you want your children to hold you in high esteem, hold them in high esteem! If you want them to listen when you speak, listen when *they* speak! Honor their right to disagree with you, and they'll be more likely to consider what you say.

III. A Couple of Practical Suggestions

Let's end our study with a few words of advice.

A. Keep the "big picture" in mind. Remember, what happens in the present stretches fingers into the future. If your decisions will affect your family, discuss them with your family. If you have been wrong, admit it. Don't let today's mistakes become tomorrow's regrets.

B. Make your Christianity easy to live with. Live your faith every day, but guard against fanatical extremes; be natural. Teach your children to know God as their friend and, as they mature, as their Lord. Talk more of God's love and holiness than His wrath and justice, and match your walk to your words.

> ### A Family Motto
>
> "Having thus a fond affection for you, we were well-pleased to impart to you not only the gospel of God but also our own lives, because you had become very dear to us" (1 Thess. 2:8).

 Living Insights

Study One

As we begin to bring our series to a close, let's review the essentials we've been discussing. Examine each principle, spending a few minutes thinking through the implications for your family. Then jot down how you could apply it to your specific family situation.

Biblical principles are more important than traditional opinions.

_____

_____

Personal relationships are more valuable than individual accomplishments.

_____

_____

Domestic priorities rate higher than church programs.

_____

_____

Positive acceptance is better reinforcement than negative reactions.

_____

_____

Unconditional forgiveness is better than lingering probation.

_____

_____

Mutual respect is of greater importance than chain of command.

_____

_____

🌹 *Living Insights*

Study Two ▬▬▬▬▬▬▬▬▬▬▬▬▬▬▬▬▬▬▬▬▬▬

Now that you've got your mind good and supple, commit to memory
1 Thessalonians 2:8.

> Having thus a fond affection for you, we were well-pleased
> to impart to you not only the gospel of God but also our
> own lives, because you had become very dear to us.

• Meditate on the passage and write down some of your observations.

_____

_____

_____

_____

What is the motive for imparting?

_____

_____

_____

Continued on next page

Practically speaking, what are some ways you can impart the gospel *and* your life to your family?

_____

_____

_____

_____

_____

_____

_____

Looking Ahead
to Things That Last

Selected Scripture

We live in a day of instant everything—from coffee to four-minute microwave cakes.

There's not much we have to wait for anymore. We can bank around the clock or shop till we drop. And with the state lotteries and publishers' sweepstakes, we can even become overnight millionaires.

From fast food to express mail, speed is a big part of our lives. But when you look back over your life, will you remember what you did ... or only that you did it *fast?*

Let's invest some of that time we keep saving in things that last—things that will live on long after those high-speed conveniences wind down. But first, let's review the things that really matter.

I. When Looking Back, These Things Matter

Our lives are crowded with things that are important. But as we learned in our last lesson, six things stand out that really matter.

—Biblical principles are more important than traditional opinions.

Personal relationships are more valuable than individual accomplishments.

—Domestic priorities rate higher than church programs.

—Positive acceptance is better reinforcement than negative reactions.

—Unconditional forgiveness is better than lingering probation.

—Mutual respect is of greater importance than chain of command.

II. When Looking Ahead, These Things Last

We've looked at the need to prioritize the things that really matter in life. But in this world of changing fads, innovative technology, and overnight obsolescence, what things can we count on to really *last?* What can we sink our souls into that we can be sure will be there tomorrow? What can we pour our hearts into that we can know won't become outdated? More than likely, those things are in our lives now—we just need to give them our attention.

A. The institutions of marriage and family will last. The past few decades have challenged the concept of marriage and rearranged the lives of families, but they haven't defeated the system. Even in an era of live-in partners and day-care children, the family is still the heart of society. It's an institution God established (Gen. 2:18–25), and what He establishes lasts.

B. God's arrangement and requirements for domestic harmony will last. God designed marriage to be a fulfilling, peaceful arrangement. Unfortunately, many homes echo with emptiness or shudder with angry shouts, and their occupants think God's plan has somehow gone awry. But it's not the recipe that's the problem—it's how the directions are being followed. Although the reasons for marital disharmony sometimes seem complicated, they can usually be boiled down to two brass-tacks issues.

    1. Someone has ignored or disobeyed God's directives. Remember the guidelines we discovered in Genesis 2:24–25?

> For this cause a man shall leave his father and his mother, and shall cleave to his wife; and they shall become one flesh. And the man and his wife were both naked and were not ashamed.

    Severance, permanence, unity, and *intimacy.* It takes all four elements to play a harmonious chord. Leave one out, and your marriage will eventually strike a sour note.

    2. Divorce has been kept as an option. God's plan is for one man to marry one woman and for them to stay married throughout life. The Bible offers few reasons for divorce, but society can think up dozens. Though the pain of divorce is incalculable—and not only to husband and wife—we still back away from God's solutions. We'd rather switch partners than fight for fidelity; we prefer to change our paths than change ourselves. If the solutions to our problems don't work fast, we don't believe they'll work at all. And when divorce becomes an option, we throw a roadblock across any avenue that might lead to a hopeful answer.

"Marriage Begins with the Vow"

    Society hurls questions at marriage like spears searching for chinks in armor. "Why worry about a document? What does a piece of paper mean, anyway? Why go through the expense and trouble of a ceremony?" Walter Wangerin, Jr., in his book *As for Me and My House,* holds up a shining shield.

> Listen: marriage begins when two people make the clear, unqualified promise to be faithful, each to the other, until the end of their days. That spoken promise makes the difference. A new relationship is initiated.

162

Marriage begins when each vows to commit herself, himself, unto the other and to no other human in this world: "I promise you my faithfulness, until death parts us." That vow, once spoken, once heard, permits a new, enduring trust: each one may trust the vow of the other one. And that vow forms the foundation of the relationship to be built upon it hereafter.

A promise made, a promise witnessed, a promise heard, remembered, and trusted —this is the groundwork of marriage. Not emotions. No, not even love. Not physical desires or personal needs or sexuality. Not the practical fact of living together. Not even the piercing foresight or some peculiar miracle of All-seeing God. Rather, a promise, a vow, makes the marriage.

"I promise you my faithfulness, until death parts us."[1]

Marriage is a matter of commitment. And it is a commitment that matters. It matters to your children. It matters to Christ. And those should be pretty good reasons to make it matter to you.

C. The effects of domestic influence will last. Childhood never leaves us. The messages we heard at home, positive or negative, are the messages some part of us still believes. One man has said that those memories are "like shrapnel embedded in flesh,"[2] never to be removed. We send lasting messages to our own children every day.

1. **Positive messages.** If you demonstrate thoughtfulness and caring, your children will carry those qualities. If you show sacrifice and servanthood, they'll remember your example. If you model masculinity or femininity, wise use of time, and strong character, your children are likely to bear your healthy image.

2. **Negative messages.** If you abuse and bring pain by neglect, your children may never quite heal. If you refuse to listen,

1. Walter Wangerin, Jr., *As for Me and My House* (Nashville, Tenn.: Thomas Nelson Publishers, 1987), p. 18.

2. Gordon MacDonald, *The Effective Father* (Wheaton, Ill.: Tyndale House Publishers, 1977), p. 68. Used by permission.

they may stop hearing. If you waver in your commitment to them, they may become insecure. If you ignore misbehavior and relax on discipline—they may develop deep-rooted character flaws.

┌─ *Following in Your Footsteps* ─────────────────────────┐
"Wear shoes you want to be filled. The beauty of Daddy's little boy clomping down the stairs with a pair of his father's shoes on is a nostalgic one. Someday he will do more than simply fill two shoes; he will fill the shoes of a way of life that he has seen in his father. At best, the effective father will have fifteen years to set the style, and the first eight are the most important. After that—and I am already being generous—we can hope at best to make minor mid-course corrections."[3]
└──┘

III. A Look Within

Let two final questions probe your heart.
A. **Are you investing in things that last?** Evaluate your priorities. Maybe it's time to shift your focus from the here-and-now to the now-and-forever.
B. **Do you realize the value of maintenance?** We sometimes spend hours maintaining our possessions—cleaning our clothes, vacuuming our rugs, changing our oil—while our families roll along day after day neglected. Isn't it time you popped the hood on that most important of possessions? Isn't it time you at least checked the oil? If it's a quart low on understanding, is it any wonder the engine makes all those annoying little noises? If it's a quart low on kindness, is it any wonder it overheats and stalls? Remember, the cost of maintaining a family—or the family car— is a lot cheaper than the cost of repair.

┌─ *A Matter of Perspective* ─────────────────────────────┐
"To keep what has been gained is not a smaller virtue than to make new acquisitions" (John Calvin).
└──┘

3. MacDonald, *The Effective Father*, p. 102. Used by permission.

Living Insights

Home is where life makes up its mind. And it makes up its mind largely based on the messages it receives there. The messages your children receive at home will be replayed throughout their entire lives, and that is what will shape them into adults.

Those messages will reverberate in their memory to tell them what masculinity is ... what femininity is ... what a husband should be ... what a wife should be ... what a parent should be ... what things in life should be valued.

The tape runs in a never-ending loop to echo every value you espouse—for better or for worse. What messages are you sending to your children? What values are they storing in their tape library?

- We often pass on the same messages to our children that we received from our parents, regardless of how distorted. In the space below, jot down a few of the messages—positive and negative—that you received from your parents. Also write down which of those you are passing down to your children. Then take a step back and see which messages need adjusting. On some, the volume may need to be turned up. On others, the message may need to be erased altogether.

Messages from My Parents   **Messages to My Children**

Positive

_____   _____

_____   _____

_____   _____

_____   _____

_____   _____

Negative

_____   _____

_____   _____

_____   _____

_____   _____

Living Insights

We've covered a lot of ground in our study of the family. We've seen the potholes that can jolt us, and we've discovered some ways to detour around them. There's a lot to remember! Let's review what we've learned and come up with some signposts to remind us where we're going.

- Look back through the last half of your study guide and reread your notes. Are there truths and applications from each lesson that stand out in your mind? Write them down in the space provided.

Wisdom Needed for Building the Structure
(Continued from Lesson 12)

What's *Right* about Adolescence? _____

_____

_____

_____

You and Your Son _____

_____

_____

_____

You and Your Daughter (Part One) _____

_____

_____

_____

You and Your Daughter (Part Two) _____

_____

_____

_____

Wisdom Claimed While Weathering the Storms

Releasing the Reins _____

_____

_____

_____

What about the Older Rebel? _____

_____

_____

_____

Equipping the Family for the Unforeseen _____

_____

_____

_____

Equipping the Family for the Unbearable _____

_____

_____

_____

Equipping the Family for the Unusual _____

_____

_____

_____

What to Do When You've Blown It _____

_____

_____

_____

Continued on next page

Looking Back on Things That Matter _____

_____

_____

_____

Looking Ahead to Things That Last _____

_____

_____

_____

Books for Probing Further

In the Old Testament the word *wisdom* describes the technical skill needed in making priestly garments (Exod. 28:3), in crafting metalwork (31:3), and in executing the strategy of battle (Isa. 10:13).

In a more general sense the word refers to the practical skill of living. The source of this skill is the all-knowing, all-powerful God of heaven. By His wisdom God numbered the clouds (Job 38:37) and established the earth (Prov. 3:19). He alone knows wisdom in its truest and most ultimate sense (Job 28:20, 23).

Proverbs tells us that the fear of the Lord is the beginning of wisdom (9:10). For only He can impart the wisdom that enables us to successfully navigate life's choppy and uncertain waters.

To chart your way around the reefs that crop up from time to time, we have included a list of books to put on your ship's manifest. May God's Word steer your course and His Spirit fill your sails as you continue to grow wise in family life.

I. Wisdom Used in Appraising the Scene

Kimmel, Tim. *Little House on the Freeway.* Portland, Oreg.: Multnomah Press, 1987. In this warm and humorous book, the author pinpoints the marks of a hurried home fast on its way to self-destruction. With practical solutions, he shows how to restore calm and rest to your family.

Schaeffer, Edith. *What Is a Family?* Old Tappan, N.J.: Fleming H. Revell Co., 1975. In appraising your family scene, probably no book will be as helpful as this one. It is a compelling mosaic of all that God intended the family to be.

II. Wisdom Applied to Cultivating the Soil

Hull, Karen. *The Mommy Book.* Grand Rapids, Mich.: Zondervan Publishing House, 1986. Karen Hull has written a practical and helpful guide for inexperienced mothers confronted by the often overwhelming demands of an infant.

MacDonald, Gordon. *The Effective Father.* Wheaton, Ill.: Tyndale House Publishers, 1977. MacDonald presents a practical and biblical approach to fatherhood in an engaging book that is full of vivid illustrations, warmth, and wisdom.

Neff, LaVonne. *One of a Kind.* Portland, Oreg.: Multnomah Press, 1988. This book will show you how understanding personality types can help you better know and appreciate yourself and your loved ones. It will also explain how your children are unique and, therefore, why your parenting style should be unique.

Swindoll, Charles R. *You and Your Child.* Nashville, Tenn.: Thomas Nelson Publishers, 1977. This book is the seedbed from which the book *Growing Wise in Family Life* took root. It contains helpful sections that deal with children who have special needs— including the adopted child, the handicapped child, and the single-parent child.

III. Wisdom Needed for Building the Structure
Dobson, James. *Dare to Discipline.* Wheaton, Ill.: Tyndale House Publishers, 1970. Everyone with children will appreciate the balance between love and control that Dobson offers here. Built on a solid biblical premise, the book is buttressed by Dobson's strong background in psychology and is replete with examples from his own case studies. It's a classic in the field of child discipline.

————. *Hide or Seek.* Revised edition. Old Tappan, N.J.: Fleming H. Revell Co., 1979. In this excellent book, Dobson exposes the false set of scales with which our society weighs individual worth. He then shows the parent and teacher how to develop a strategy for cultivating self-esteem in children. This book will do more than help you understand your child; it will help you understand yourself and the forces that shaped you into the person you are today.

Peterson, Eugene H. *Growing Up with Your Teenager.* Old Tappan, N.J.: Fleming H. Revell, 1987. Peterson is one of the most insightful writers of our day. In this book he shows how to promote an atmosphere of communication, growth, honesty, forgiveness, and love between parents and adolescents. The study questions at the end of each chapter make the book particularly appealing for group discussion.

Smalley, Gary. *The Key to Your Child's Heart.* Waco, Tex.: Word Books, 1984. This book centers around the principle of keeping your child's spirit open. Sharing frankly from his own family's experience, Smalley recounts what has and has not worked in his home and includes ways to draw your own family closer together.

IV. Wisdom Claimed While Weathering the Storms
Smalley, Gary and John Trent. *The Blessing.* Nashville, Tenn.: Thomas Nelson Publishers, 1986. Our emotional and psychological make-up cries out for what the Bible calls "the blessing"—the knowledge that a parental figure loves and accepts us unconditionally. The authors detail the five elements of the blessing, how to bless

others, and how to recover from growing up in a family where the blessing was withheld.

————. *The Language of Love.* Pomona, Calif.: Focus on the Family Publishing, 1988. This excellent new book explores "emotional word pictures": a time-tested method of bridging the communication gaps that may exist between you and the people you love.

White, John. *Parents in Pain.* Downers Grove, Ill.: InterVarsity Press, 1979. This respected writer and former professor of psychiatry offers comfort and counsel to parents of children struggling with severe problems such as alcoholism, homosexuality, and suicide. With practical suggestions he helps parents deal with their feelings and guides them through the disorienting maze of parental pain.

Insight for Living
Cassette Tapes
GROWING WISE IN FAMILY LIFE

You don't have to look far these days for advice about family living. But not all advice is worth heeding, especially when it discounts God's timeless wisdom. Here is a Bible-based study that is filled with practical suggestions designed to strengthen your family ties.

			U.S.	Canada
GWF	CS	Cassette series—includes album cover	$65.25	$83.00
		Individual cassettes—include messages		
		A and B	5.00	6.35

These prices are effective as of December 1988 and are subject to change without notice.

GWF   1-A: *Danger Signals of a Disintegrating Family*—1 Samuel 1–4
        B: *Is Yours a Genuinely Christian Family?*—Deuteronomy 6:1–24

GWF   2-A: *Dads, Front and Center*—1 Thessalonians 2:8–12
        B: *Mothers: An Endangered Species*—Proverbs 24:3–4,
            2 Timothy 1:1–7

GWF   3-A: *Mom and Dad . . . Meet Your Child*—Proverbs 22:6
        B: *The Bents in Your Baby*—Proverbs 22:6, Psalm 139

GWF   4-A: *A Chip off the Old Bent*—Exodus 34:5–8
        B: *When Brothers and Sisters Battle*—Selected Scripture

GWF   5-A: *Shaping the Will with Wisdom*—Selected Proverbs
        B: *Ways to Enhance Esteem*—Ephesians 5:25–30, Selected Proverbs

GWF   6-A: *Change: Challenging Years of Adolescence*—Selected Scripture
        B: *Another Look at Adolescence*—2 Chronicles 34:1–21, Daniel 1:3–20

GWF   7-A: *What's Right about Adolescence?*—Selected Scripture
        B: *You and Your Son*—Selected Proverbs

GWF   8-A: *You and Your Daughter (Part One)*—Selected Proverbs
        B: *You and Your Daughter (Part Two)*—Selected Proverbs

GWF   9-A: *Releasing the Reins*—Ephesians 4:11–16
        B: *What about the Older Rebel?*—Luke 15:11–24

GWF 10-A: *Equipping the Family for the Unforeseen*—Job 1–2
        B: *Equipping the Family for the Unbearable*—2 Samuel 18:5–19:8

GWF 11-A: *Equipping the Family for the Unusual*—Genesis 6–9, Hebrews 11:7
        B: *What to Do When You've Blown It*—Selected Scripture

GWF 12-A: *Looking Back on Things That Matter*—Selected Scripture
        B: *Looking Ahead to Things That Last*—Selected Scripture

How to Order by Mail

Simply mark on the order form whether you want the series or individual tapes. Mail the form with your payment to the appropriate address listed below. We will process your order as promptly as we can.

United States: Mail your order to the Sales Department at Insight for Living, Post Office Box 4444, Fullerton, California 92634. If you wish your order to be shipped first-class for faster delivery, add 10 percent of the total order amount (not including California sales tax). Otherwise, please allow four to six weeks for delivery by fourth-class mail. We accept personal checks, money orders, Visa, and MasterCard in payment for materials. Unfortunately, we are unable to offer invoicing or COD orders.

Canada: Mail your order to Insight for Living Ministries, Post Office Box 2510, Vancouver, British Columbia V6B 3W7. Please add 7 percent of your total order for first-class postage and allow approximately four weeks for delivery. Our listeners in British Columbia must also add a 6 percent sales tax to the total of all tape orders (not including postage). We accept personal checks, money orders, Visa, or MasterCard in payment for materials. Unfortunately, we are unable to offer invoicing or COD orders.

Australia, New Zealand, or Papua New Guinea: Mail your order to Insight for Living, Inc., GPO Box 2823 EE, Melbourne, Victoria 3001, Australia. Please allow six to ten weeks for delivery by surface mail. If you would like your order sent airmail, the delivery time may be reduced. Whether you choose surface or airmail, postage costs must be added to the amount of purchase and included with your order. Please use the chart that follows to determine correct postage. Due to fluctuating currency rates, we can accept only personal checks made payable in U.S. funds, international money orders, Visa, or MasterCard in payment for materials.

Overseas: Other overseas residents should contact our U.S. office. Please allow six to ten weeks for delivery by surface mail. If you would like your order sent airmail, the delivery time may be reduced. Whether you choose surface or airmail, postage costs must be added to the amount of purchase and included with your order. Please use the chart that follows to determine correct postage. Due to fluctuating currency rates, we can accept only personal checks made payable in U.S. funds, international money orders, Visa, or MasterCard in payment for materials.

Type of Postage	Cassettes
Surface	10% of total order
Airmail	25% of total order

For Faster Service, Order by Telephone

To purchase using Visa or MasterCard, you are welcome to use our **toll-free** numbers between the hours of 8:30 A.M. and 4:00 P.M., Pacific time, Monday through Friday. The number to call from anywhere in the United States is **1-800-772-8888**. To order from Canada, call our Vancouver office at **1-800-663-7639.** Vancouver residents should call (604) 272-5811. Telephone orders from overseas are handled through our Sales Department at (714) 870-9161. We are unable to accept collect calls.

Our Guarantee

Our cassettes are guaranteed for ninety days against faulty performance or breakage due to a defect in the tape. For best results, please be sure your tape recorder is in good operating condition and is cleaned regularly.

Note: To cover processing and handling, there is a $10 fee for *any* returned check.

Order Form

Please send me the following cassette tapes:

The current series: ☐ GWF CS *Growing Wise in Family Life*

Individual tapes:
☐ GWF 1   ☐ GWF 4   ☐ GWF 7   ☐ GWF 10
☐ GWF 2   ☐ GWF 5   ☐ GWF 8   ☐ GWF 11
☐ GWF 3   ☐ GWF 6   ☐ GWF 9   ☐ GWF 12

I am enclosing:

$ _____ To purchase the cassette series for $65.25 (in Canada $83.00*) which includes the album cover

$ _____ To purchase individual tapes at $5.00 each (in Canada $6.35*)

$ _____ Total of purchases

$ _____ If the order will be delivered in California, please add 6 percent sales tax

$ _____ U.S. residents please add 10 percent for first-class shipping and handling if desired

$ _____ *British Columbia residents please add 6 percent sales tax

$ _____ Canadian residents please add 7 percent for postage

$ _____ **Overseas residents please add appropriate postage** (See postage chart under "How to Order by Mail.")

$ _____ As a gift to the Insight for Living radio ministry for which a tax-deductible receipt will be issued

$ _____ Total amount due (Please do not send cash.)

Form of payment:

☐ Check or money order made payable to Insight for Living
☐ Credit card (Visa or MasterCard only)
If there is a balance: ☐ apply it as a donation   ☐ please refund

---

Credit card purchases:
☐ Visa   ☐ MasterCard Number _____
Expiration Date _____
Signature _____
We cannot process your credit card purchase without your signature.

Name _____

Address _____

_____

City _____

State/Province _____ Zip/Postal Code _____

Country _____

Telephone (_____) _____ Radio Station __ __ __ __

Should questions arise concerning your order, we may need to contact you.